Apparitions
and
Survival of Death

By RAYMOND BAYLESS

With a Foreword by D. Scott Rogo

A CITADEL PRESS BOOK
Published by Carol Publishing Group

Other Books by the Author

THE ENIGMA OF THE POLTERGEIST

ANIMAL GHOSTS

THE OTHER SIDE OF DEATH

EXPERIENCES OF A PSYCHICAL RESEARCHER

CONTENTS

**Dedicated to my wife, Marjorie,
who has shared many
psychical adventures
with me**

FOREWORD

IT CAN rightly be said that psychical research is the study of death. While religion outlines teachings about death, and psychology tries to prepare us for this final adventure, it is psychical research which comes to grips with the one central question that all other sciences ignore: Is there some component of the personality or component of the physical organism that survives death? Likewise, we must also ask, can this surviving entity communicate thoughts, emotions, and information to the living?

One of the subjects that throws important light on these questions is the study of apparitions. Historically there have been many attempts to construct theoretical models to explain these mysterious phantoms which sometimes appear to friends and relatives miles away at the time of their own deaths and have been seen collectively by many witnesses. These same hypotheses also try to explain how apparitions can or cannot aid in our understanding of the mystery of death. Some of these theories explain the apparitions as being "unreal" in the physical sense and claim they are "telepathic hallucinations." The percipient, receiving a telepathic signal, translates it into a visual hallucination. Unfortunately, this theory does not explain why apparitions can move physical objects. Other theories explain the apparition as being semiphysical and some type of "force" which is liberated from the body at death. But why do apparitions, far from the popular conception of the misty white figure, appear dressed in everyday clothes? Here again we find that the propounded theory is contradicted by observed data.

It is to this problem that Raymond Bayless directs this book. Instead of presenting just another collection of ghost stories, as books on this subject often are, Mr. Bayless tries to update the theories by disqualifying the "classical," and I might add inadequate, theories about apparitions. In their place he proposes new models for explanation, using a wealth of cases as evidence.

The critical point in the study of apparitions is the fact that apparitions of the living are seen just as often as apparitions of the dead. Obviously, a general theory must take into account this realm of case material. One researcher who did just this was the late Professor Hornell Hart who, in cooperation with a group of collaborators, wrote his masterly "Six Theories about Apparitions," published by the Society for Psychical Research. In this work Hart showed how apparitions of the living and of the dead appear to be of the same nature. He, like Mr. Bayless, also saw the inadequacies of conventional theories and set about constructing new ones. But, if this has already been done, why the need for this current book? Toward the end of his life Hart revised his thinking in the light of the breakthroughs of Dr. Robert Crookall, a British scientist studying the out-of-the-body experience (more popularly called astral projection), who presented a depth of meaning and understanding about "apparitions of the living" never before discovered. Hart's last contribution to psychical research was an article, "Scientific Survival Research," published in the *International Journal of Parapsychology*, which stressed the importance of Crookall's work.

Before Hart's death he had written a complete draft of a book synthesizing his work with Crookall's. This work remains unpublished and virtually unknown.

The need for and importance of Mr. Bayless's book is just this synthesis. In this present volume he coordinates Hornell Hart's contributions to our study of apparitions with the critical revisions necessary in the light of Dr. Crookall's work. This is not to say that the present volume is overly pedagogical; for Mr. Bayless has interspersed these theories with numerous cases and facts about psychical phenomena in a very readable manner. However, scholarship is never sacrificed.

Like both Hornell Hart and Robert Crookall, Raymond Bayless sees that apparitions serve as strong evidence for man's survival of death, and his book is a welcome addition to the literature on the subject.

D. Scott Rogo

PREFACE

WITH this survey of apparitions and apparitional activities, I have attempted to give a picture not only of the more "conventional" phantom, but also a view of more exotic phenomena such as those witnessed and chronicled by the Reverend Charles L. Tweedale. The interpretation of apparitional phenomena presented is based upon the theories of Dr. Robert Crookall and Professor Hornell Hart. Both authorities admit that in certain cases phantoms are semiphysical in nature and are capable of producing raps, moving objects, and other effects of a like order. The theories of these two men have resolved many apparent contradictions found with apparitional activity and have replaced, in large measure, previous telepathic concepts with consistent and thoroughly workable schematics.

Apparitional phenomena cannot be viewed apart from the other great categories of psychical phenomena: mediumistic communications, "physical" phenomena, haunting and poltergeist manifestations, cross-correspondences, and, in short, the entire psychical realm. The sum total of this vast panorama of psychism results in only one workable theory which can accommodate all types of phenomena, and that theory is built upon the principle of survival of death.

Apparitional effects, in large degree, provide obvious and enormously important evidence representing survival of

11

death, and as such furnish a fascinating and tremendously significant field of study.

Individual cases and even collections of cases differ in degree of strength of evidence, but, in spite of this variance, all fit smoothly into an over-all, self-consistent pattern. As always, the original records with their verifying material should be consulted for a more detailed study.

CHAPTER ONE

GENERAL

CONSIDERATIONS

THE STUDY of phantoms is truly a special division of psychical research and offers a vast field containing a rich yield of paranormal phenomena running the entire gamut of psychism. Of this there is no doubt; the researcher need have no fears of lacking material both historical and contemporary for analysis.

Today the bookshelves are filled with many books, both paperback and hard cover, containing accounts of presumed psychical happenings. Some are interesting, some have definite value, but many are utterly worthless—filled with tales of ghosts and hauntings which are entertaining, it is true, but lacking in any proper factual background.

This flood of popular literature devoted to psychism has many drawbacks as well as some advantages. At least, the public's mind is drawn to the field and it has become obvious that the subject is not totally unrespectable with intelligent people. However, to my mind, this advantage, if advantage it really is, is outweighed by the real harm, scientifically speaking, such books engender.

For example, I have a paperback in front of me which is described as a best-seller—a worthless distinction except financially speaking. In a chapter given over to tales of hauntings are a number of stories, presumably told to the author, including one account which tells how an invisible ghost helped a man put on his coat! How helpful!

Another tale tells of a house once owned by a smuggler which has a ghost who walks during the full moon and disappears after transmuting into a sphere of fire. How silly! No documentation, as usual, is provided. Story after story of a more or less ridiculous nature is recounted, all without verifying evidence, and consequently without any value whatsoever to parapsychological science. But possibly, on very rare occasions, some of these tales picture genuine hauntings, and this is the rub. These stories which, in spite of their lack of verification, are genuine are swallowed up in the morass of worthless accounts invented for popular consumption.

Because a few real accounts are mixed with a potpourri of silly ghost stories (some lacking any semblance of reality), the public is provided with a false picture of psychic phenomena. This distorted view in no way aids either its understanding or helps scientific progress in a field admittedly possessing subtle difficulties enough as is. I greatly regret this flood of dubious and valueless material.

Why are such stories invented? There are several reasons. The primary one, one popular with professional writers, is simply money! The professional writer, realizing that phantoms are a popular subject at the moment, may sit before a typewriter and, as with any other tale, simply invent a ghost story—a good, lively haunting filled with action and eerie drama. Another method very prevalent is to record a story told by an individual, minus, of course, any verification, and present it as a factual account. This, unfortunately, is a very widely used procedure. Needless to say, the original account may become very changed when it finally sees print. Not too long ago, I talked to a woman who had told a well-known "ghost chaser" a tale of haunting, which, when it reached print, was most remarkably altered. But from the author's standpoint in such cases monèy is the motive.

Why do private individuals or even families invent such tales? The reasons here are mixed and at times quite murky, generally with psychological overtones. Some people will deliberately write a false story to sell to a magazine. This occurs frequently, I am sure.

In the course of my parapsychological investigations, I have studied many cases of presumed haunting. With the exception of poltergeist cases (a subtle distinction which will be discussed later), I have encountered more than one example which presented excellent evidence showing the presence of genuine psychical phenomena. However, the usual example involved a person or persons who had "invented" a case for one reason or another. It must always be remembered that cases involving real haunting phenomena are extremely rare, and are not to be found in the numbers that many amateur investigators fondly believe.

I have met with instances where the children were fooling their parents. In cases of this type, excitement and personal attention are gained. I have been present during cases which were resolved easily—examples in which the adult members of the family were creating a haunting (verbally, of course) for the purpose of receiving attention. I do think that the desire for excitement and attention enters strongly into examples of this type, just as it does where children are concerned.

So it can easily be seen that the motives for inventing cases of haunting are not too many in number. In fact, it can generally be said that excitement, attention, and money are the primary reasons behind false tales of ghosts and hauntings.

There are, to offset the deluge of dubious and worthless books that are unfortunately easily available, a number of good and valuable works which have been written by reputable psychical researchers, some of great fame and scientific attainment. To list just a few, there are: *Ghosts and Poltergeists* by Father Herbert Thurston, *Haunted Houses* by Professor Camille Flammarion, *Can We Explain the Poltergeist?* by A. R. G. Owen, *Poltergeist over England* by Harry Price, *Haunted People: The Story of the Poltergeist Down the Centuries* by Hereward Carrington and Dr. Nandor Fodor, *The Psychic in the House* by Dr. Walter Franklin Prince, *The Most Haunted House in England* and *The End of Borley Rectory* by Harry Price, and *The Snettisham Ghost* by the Reverend Rowland W. Maitland (which is a more complete account of a noted haunting case that F. W. H. Myers included in his paper, "The Subliminal Self"). This case was also discussed to some degree by Abdy Collins in *The Cheltenham Ghost*. A book commonly considered a "classic" on the subject of ghosts and hauntings is *Apparitions* by G. N. M. Tyrrell. (In the case of Tyrrell, I must admit that I believe his fundamental proposition to be in error.) There are other good works on this general subject, but this list will suffice for the moment.[1]

Now the question of the reality of ghosts and hauntings must be dealt with. In general, I believe it is safe to say that the public does not realize the vast amount of respectable evidence which has been amassed testifying to the reality of such psychical phenomena.

[1] Some years ago, I wrote a book on this general subject called *The Enigma of the Poltergeist*.

One of the very first facets of psychism to be studied by the Society for Psychical Research, which was established in 1882 as a result of a proposal for its creation by Sir William Barrett, was the study of apparitions. It was immediately realized that a large number of apparitions, which had been observed by perfectly normal and healthy individuals, represented people who had just died. Other examples represented people just before or some time after death. Eventually, an over-all classification of apparitions was created. These consisted of phantoms of the living, of the dying, and of the dead.

In the case of apparitions of the living, it was soon found that they represented individuals quite alive, but perhaps in a state of trance, ill, or even simply sleeping.

In the case of phantasms of the dying, phantoms were included which coincided with the act of death.

And in the case of phantoms representing the dead, it was discovered that many were observed usually in one area or house, which of course put them into the category of hauntings.

The monumental *Phantasms of the Living*, authored by three pioneers of the past, Edmund Gurney, Frederic W. H. Myers, and Frank Podmore, published in the year 1886, includes many of the earlier findings of the Society for Psychical Research. Due to a prevailing inclination toward an explanation of telepathic mechanisms for most psychical phenomena, and perhaps an overlying unscientific bias against the physical phenomena of psychism, it was stated that a prima facie case for the existence of telepathy had been established. Further similar works followed: the *Census of Hallucinations* in Vol. X, 1894, of the *Proceedings* of the

Society, and a succeeding *Phantasms of the Living* by Eleanor M. Sidgwick. Gurney stated in Chapter Two, entitled, "The Theory of Chance-Coincidence," of *Phantasms of the Living* that the author's belief "that our collection comprises a large number of coincidences which have some other cause than chance will still, I believe, be amply justified."

I am sure that anyone who reads the collection of cases in *Phantasms of the Living*, plus other collections of similar examples, will come to exactly the same conclusion advanced by Myers, Gurney, and Podmore that such phenomena definitely exist.

Professor Camille Flammarion compiled a large collection of supernormal incidents—a great many of which featured phantoms and haunting phenomena. His famous book, *The Unknown*, includes cases of apparitions, etc., as well as his noted trilogy, *Death and Its Mystery*, composed of three volumes entitled *Before Death, At the Moment of Death*, and *After Death.* His *Haunted Houses*, mentioned previously, is, of course, devoted to haunting phenomena. Flammarion's large collection of cases is immensely impressive, particularly when compared with the multitude of similar cases collected over the years.

Naturally, many cases of haunting and poltergeist phenomena, which for the time I lump together, are to be found in the various works devoted to this general field.

Still other collections of like cases exist, and both the Society for Psychical Research and the American Society for Psychical Research have, over the many years of their existence, gathered a large and significant harvest of haunting and apparitional cases.

As a result of this truly immense amount of material testifying to the existence of hauntings and ghosts, it is, I am thoroughly convinced, impossible except for the hopelessly biased or the uninformed to resist the admission that such phenomena are completely factual.

Few parapsychologists today will deny the existence of such psychical manifestations, and those few who still refuse to admit the obvious simply have no business being involved in the field of psychical research, or, if you wish, parapsychology. I can only suggest that they display their talents in other fields more befitting. Plumbing, for instance, is not overly abstract in its conceptual structure and would do very nicely. Besides, it pays better.

Apparitions can be placed in various groups. G. N. M. Tyrrell refers to four general classes: First, apparitions of the living, which represent phantoms which were produced deliberately and experimentally. This class must also fall into the category of "astral projection" or out-of-the-body experiences. The second type includes apparitions which are sensed, which represent a living person who has experienced a crisis of some order. Again, this group falls also into the category of astral projection. A third group is comprised of apparitions which are seen of a person who is recognized long after death. In cases of this type, a crisis does not seem to play any part. The last group contains those traditional players in legend and Gothic tale, ghosts. The ghost as such is associated with a particular place, building, ship, home, and so on.

Tyrrell does note that there are other types of apparitions which really do not fit into any of the above groups. Unrecognized phantoms which may be seen only once represent one type, and I will add that animal apparitions are another.

Disputed apparitions of scenery, at times with accompanying figures, would be still another.

And with these observations offered by Tyrrell, the examination of apparitional data can begin.

CHAPTER TWO

OBJECTIVE

PHANTOMS

BEFORE plunging into this fascinating subject, I must again remark that the factual nature of apparitions is solidly established and beyond all reasonable doubt. The burden of proof is no longer upon the shoulders of those who affirm the existence of apparitional activity—and psychical phenomena in general—but rests firmly upon the shoulders of those who would deny it.

In my case, my acceptance does not rely alone upon the overwhelming evidence testifying to the existence of phantoms—sufficient reason in itself—for I have had the very good fortune to have observed an apparition and clearly must accept the existence of such phenomena from personal experience.

Prior to the inception of scientific psychical research, which for all practical purpose took place in the first half of the nineteenth century, a number of views were advanced regarding the nature of apparitions. Most were "naïve," and were the result of a lack of evidence which we would consider valid. However, some observations of the earlier periods were perfectly valid, but, in spite of legitimate cases of psychical activity, superstition played a deadly role. The all-pervading belief in the reality of witchcraft cast the minds of most in a rigid pattern which excluded the type of views found today, and the lack of knowledge of subconscious activities further firmed the pattern.

However, the scientific spirit was not totally lacking in earlier days despite less psychological knowledge. As Harry Price noted in *Poltergeist over England*, the Reverend Joseph Glanvil, who published an account of the famed Drummer of Tedworth poltergeist disturbance in 1666, showed a definite scientific attitude in the final comments of his paper, "Philosophical Considerations Concerning the Existence of Sorcerers and Sorcery." This attitude paralleled the modern regard for worthy evidence and can be clearly seen in spite of his wholehearted belief in the immanence of Satan and his diabolic cohorts.

In his paper, the Reverend Glanvil comments that he has related the essentials of the disturbance (the Tedworth poltergeist case) including certain incidents in some detail. He also notes significantly that the phenomena which he chronicled were not as bizarre as events given in popular ghost stories. This very lack of extravagant features tells strongly in favor of their actuality. Yet the phenomena observed, so very strange and truly grotesque and apparently even dangerous, show that a paranormal source must clearly have been at work. The Reverend Glanvil further insists that this very strangeness indicates that spirits do at times enter into the happenings of our world. These incidents, he notes, were not reported in an uncivilized age, or with a barbaric people, or witnessed only by those prey to superstition, or of unsettled mind, or by those wishing to turn such tales to their interests. Nor were they reported merely once or twice but, instead, occurred at all times, over a long period of time, witnessed by a great number of people competent of mind in a modern and skeptical age.

The Reverend Glanvil sums up this last statement with the observation that such characteristics must cause the logical reader to admit their reality in spite of their oddity and departure from the normal course of events.

Now I do believe that this "credo" is very sensible and thoroughly intelligently put, and is, as Harry Price commented, of a modern note worthy of a serious psychical researcher. Interestingly and significantly it also demonstrates, I believe, that many of our ancestors who had imbibed deeply of the belief in black sorcery and malignant, corrupting spirits of evil, were not credulous dupes, as popular, contemporary lore would have it, but were shrewd, penetrating thinkers with a discerning eye for factual evidence.

They were betrayed, unfortunately, by a fatal lack of essential psychological knowledge which, as mentioned, was the absence of the concept of subconscious activity. Not realizing that these functions frequently ape malignant forces, and faced with the reality of haunting and poltergeist phenomena, they could of necessity only postulate the presence of spirits manifestly evil.

To discuss this point further for the moment, I have frequently been contacted by individuals who were firmly convinced that they were under siege by demonic forces. Not all of these disturbed victims were foolish or insane—far from it —but the one primary fact that they did not realize, at least to its fullest, is the incredible ability of subconscious functions to mimic paranormal forces. Naturally, many of those who have contacted me were lacking in essential psychological knowledge, and others were insufficiently educated or mentally awry. And I must add that education in itself is no guard against falling prey to various misconceptions, many of great personal harm.

During what can be termed the *Phantasms of the Living* era, psychical researchers chose to consider a telephathic mechanism as the origin of phantoms. It was felt that resistance to the concept of psychical phenomena (such as telepathy and clairvoyance) was too strong, as it was, without bringing into the picture disreputable "spiritualistic" effects such as telekinesis, paranormal raps, lights, odors, and materializations, which could only be spoken about in hushed whispers in the very respectable and very conservative rooms of organized psychical research. In consequence, telepathy was the favored subject of experimentation. Spontaneous incidents and all phantasmic manifestations (ghosts, hauntings, etc.) were usually ascribed to this cause.

In 1888 F. W. H. Myers theorized that phantoms, representing both the living and the dead, were telepathic in origin. Simply put, this theory suggests that a person involved in some type of crisis (the agent) broadcasts a telepathic message to the receiver (the percipient) who in turn casts the impulse into tangible form. That is, his mind turns the original telepathic impulse into a visually perceived but hallucinatory phantasm; or into a sound such as a voice, footsteps, a touch of a hand; or into the form of a significant odor. Some form of this theory is to this day probably held by most parapsychologists.

Myers was not consistent in his interpretation of ghostly phenomena, for he also put forth the explanation that in the case of an apparition a "psychical invasion" took place and that a "phantasmogenetic center" was established in the area around a phantom. With these rather murky words, Myers suggested that phantoms might also be partially objective in nature and as such occupy physical space. In other words, he believed that ghosts were not necessarily the result of telepathy but were to some degree objective and space-occupying in their "construction." However, in the case of collectively viewed phantasms his telepathic theory came a cropper.

Edmund Gurney, Myers's cohort, plunged into the fray to rescue, as he hoped, the telepathic theory from the "collective dilemma." He rejected the thought that phantoms are even partially objective in nature and suggested the telepathic "infection" theory, realizing that collectively perceived apparitions (phantoms seen by more than one person) placed a serious obstacle in the path of acceptance of the telepathic origin of phantoms. He did not wish to believe that they were physical or semiphysical in nature or occupied space. He thought that the suggestion—that the agent sent out the original telepathic impulse, which was then received by each percipient individually and subsequently cast into the form of a visual ghost by subconscious manipulation—was entirely too improbable to be considered.

He preferred to believe that, after the original "broadcast" was received by the primary percipient, this receiver in turn emitted another telepathic transmission, which was then picked up by still another percipient. In the case of multiple percipients the telepathic "infection," as Gurney termed it, became quite complex, unwieldy, and very improbable!

Myers did not care for this theory and objected that no evidence existed which indicated that "normal or non-paranormal hallucinations spread in this fashion." Gurney, realizing that Myers's objection was formidable, modified his thought slightly and, to my mind, inadequately. Indeed, as G. N. M. Tyrrell notes, Gurney did not seem to be overly happy with his modification or even his general theory.

Concerning the argument that a telepathic transmission can be deferred and held in latent form, F. B. Doveton wrote in the *Journal*: S.P.R., March, 1894, that the cerebral development of dogs and cats and horses, for example, is hardly complex enough to receive a telepathic transmission and then store it, so to speak, as a deferred latent impression as postulated. This point is an important one and I must admit that I cannot easily encompass the thought that my cats might receive a telepathic impression and then store it within their minds to release it later as, say, a visual hallucination— a ghost.

The editor of the *Journal* preferred not to meet this point head on. He merely replied that evidence for the seeing of apparitions by animals was meager compared with the evidence indicating that humans frequently observe phantoms. Hence, no safe conclusions could be drawn.

In 1942 G. N. M. Tyrrell, in a memorial lecture, discussed apparitions and delivered himself of a most subtle version of Gurney's theories which, to this day, is admittedly not fully understood by numerous psychical researchers. Essentially, this theory insists that a partnership is formed by the person who projects the original telepathic impulse and the receiver. Professor Hornell Hart briefly defines Tyrrell's supposition by stating that a ghost is the result of a mingling of the subconscious minds of both agent and percipient, and that the actual apparition is a kind of three-dimensional picture in motion. Tyrrell refers to "the stage carpenter" (meaning, I believe, his ability to create illusion) and other subtleties which have provided much bewilderment among parapsychologists. In essence, after trimming away certain verbal foliage, I fail to see that he said anything drastically different from what Edmund Gurney postulated. In spite of Tyrrell's preference for nonobjective phantoms, he did admit that in certain cases of poltergeists there was some evidence which argued for objective apparitions.

I find this admission an interesting exception to his beliefs, and it does seem to suggest that, like Gurney, he was not fully satisfied with his suppositions.

Other psychists, however, prefer to believe that ghosts are, at the very least, partially physical in nature and reject the suggestions of those who insist that some version of the telepathic-hallucination theory is correct for all phantoms.

For example, Professor C. J. Ducasse accepted the reality of the phenomenon known as astral projection, which is dubbed by some parapsychologists as ESP projection or out-of-the-body experience, and referring to the occasionally visible phantom of the projector, wrote that such "beings" are true space-occupying entities quite apart from and independent of their viewers. As the title, *Phantasms of the Living*, insists, "astral projections" are simply apparitions or ghosts of the living.

Dr. C. E. M. Joad wrote, in *The Recovery of Belief*, that animals have seen phantoms before their human companions saw them. This fact clearly argues for the objective nature of apparitions and shows that they were independent of their accompanying human percipients. Dr. Joad further stated that apparitions are physical objects in that the optic nerves of the viewers are activated by space-occupying and modifying phenomena.

In his book, *Loaves and Fishes*, Hereward Carrington wrote that probably the greater number of apparitions are not objective but are, in reality, "mental" or subjective in their nature. He did, however, admit that certain examples are not fully covered by this theory. In fact, he wrote that in some cases the clothing worn by apparitions might really be a "quasi-material."

It is incredible that the question of the objectivity—the physical reality—of phantoms has been fought over for so many years, and for the life of me I do not see why this battle has continued in view of the considerable evidence testifying to their objectivity in some cases.

One comparatively recent theory which indirectly insists that phantoms cannot be in any sense objective is favored by Gardner Murphy and others, who advance the suggestion that phantoms are generated by the viewer. Needless to say, if this hypothesis should be correct, apparitions and apparitional activity are obviously purely mental constructs, hallucinations of a kind, possessing no physical characteristics whatsoever. However, does not such an argument favor putting the cart before the horse?

Professor Hart in "Scientific Survival Research," published in the *International Journal of Parapsychology*, March, 1967, comments that collectively perceived apparitions cannot be considered to have been produced by their viewers for two primary reasons. One is that, with examples which included more than one possible witness, between one third and two thirds of all phantoms are collectively seen. He notes that each viewer observed the phantoms according to correct perspective; the percipients do not disagree regarding phantasmic actions, the garb, and the appearance of the apparitions; each percipient saw the apparitions when moving about according to normal parallax and perspective, and when a viewer walked around a phantom (which has occurred in a few cases) it was again seen according to normal perspective and appropriate parallax according to the point of angle.

The second reason is that which he titles "conscious apparitions of living persons": astral doubles which are clearly not created by the viewers. Cases where conscious doubles have been seen by witnesses can hardly be explained away by calling them hallucinations generated by the percipients. Cases where the projectors saw their own bodies and subsequently provided other veridical evidence testifying to the reality of the "astral excursion" can also hardly be explained away by the theory of self-generated hallucinations.

Both primary reasons given by Professor Hart cancel this old theory (which has its back where its face should be) and they present highly significant evidence demonstrating the objectivity and independence of a certain class of apparitions—both of the living and of the dead.

Professor Hart in "Six Theories about Apparitions" and in his book, *The Enigma of Survival*, also presents these various reasons as to why apparitions of an objective order cannot be counterexplained by the hallucination speculation.

Numerous cases of apparitions have furnished evidence of their objectivity, and a number of cases presenting such evidence will be described.

A famed case noted by Professor Hart, which featured a collectively witnessed apparition and which was seen according to the correct laws of parallax and perspective, originally appeared in the *Journal: S.P.R.*, November, 1893, as Case G 241. To outline this case briefly, Lady B. and her daughter were awakened during the night and saw a woman's figure in white before a fireplace. Above the fireplace was a mirror. The head of the phantom, which was reflected by the mirror, was seen in quarter profile by Lady B., and its reflection was obscured by Lady B.'s daughter, who saw the phantom's back. Its face, of course, was seen by her in the mirror. Both women leaped out of bed but by that time the phantom had disappeared.

As Professor Hart states, the various views of the apparition, including the reflection in the mirror, were seen in complete accordance with what should have been seen if the figure had been that of a living person. Further, the double sighting of the figure, a collective viewing, also argues for its independence from its viewers and indicates that it did possess some degree of objectivity, not to speak of the fact that it was reflected into a mirror.

Another remarkable, collectively perceived apparitional case is also noted by Professor Hart to illustrate his point that to invoke the theory of self-generated phantoms à la Murphy, *et al.,* or the murky theory of hallucinations via the mysterious "stage carpenter" invoked by Tyrrell, or telepathic theories in general, is to ignore facts and fly in the face of common-sense realism. This case describes the apparitional appearance of Samuel Bull and was originally reported in the *Journal: S.P.R.*, Vol. XXVII, 1932, pp. 297–304. It is an example of great significance and interest.

Briefly, Samuel Bull died in June, 1931, and his aged wife stayed on in their cottage with her grandson, James Bull. In

August, 1931, her married daughter with her husband and five children joined Mrs. Bull in her home.

About February, 1932, the daughter, Mrs. Edwards, saw a phantom of the dead man ascend a staircase and apparently walk through a closed door into the room in which he had died. James Bull also almost immediately saw the apparition. Eventually, the entire family witnessed the phantom. Mrs. Edwards's five-year-old daughter, it was recorded, recognized the apparition and called "it" by name—"Grandpa Bull." The apparition continued to be seen many times until about April 9th. Professor Hart particularly notes that, when it was sighted, all those present saw it.

A collective sighting of an apparition of such an "intense" nature obviously cannot be explained by the suggestion that it was created by the percipient as a visual hallucination responding to emotional needs, etc., etc., etc. In a case of this sort, there would be entirely too many percipients generating their own phantoms to be sensible. To endorse this theory is to violate the scientific law of parsimony, to ignore totally the obvious explanation, and abandon all common sense.

At one time Tyrrell postulated the "perfect apparition" as being one that a witness could walk around. Professor Hart in "Six Theories about Apparitions," *Proceedings*: S.P.R., Vol. 50, Part 185, May, 1956, gave a well-known case of witnessing the "perfect apparition." The case originally appeared in *Phantasms of the Living*, Vol. 1, pp. 212–14.

After work, as Alfred Bard was returning home by passing through a churchyard, he saw in front of a vault, leaning on its railing, the figure of Mrs. de Freville. She was dressed normally, but her face seemed to be unusually white in appearance. As he walked around the vault he noticed that the figure kept watching him, turning its head in order to follow his progress. He stumbled, looking away momentarily, and when he returned his gaze to where the figure had been, he saw that it had disappeared. The following morning he was told that Mrs. de Freville had died about two hours before he had seen her phantom. Interestingly, she had, in life, been greatly interested in tombs.

As in the case of Lady B. and her daughter, this apparition too was seen in correct perspective, thus fulfilling Tyrrell's demand. Further, the phantom, by following Mr. Bard with its gaze as he walked around it, showed that it was not merely a mindless automaton but possessed awareness of its viewer.

Professor Hart, in referring to the theories which were based upon Edmund Gurney's original telepathic hypothesis, finally culminating in Tyrrell's all-inclusive theory of complete hallucination of all the senses, and the speculation that the viewers of apparitions generate the phenomena according to his awareness of what expectations might reside in the agent, pointed out the fundamental errors of such views in his "Psychical Research and the Methods of Science," *Journal*: A.S.P.R., July, 1957. He listed on page 98 several reasons that certain phantoms and their "accessories" are partially objective in their structure:

> Apparitions are frequently said to have been perfectly realistic in their appearance.
> Apparitions have frequently been seen according to the principles of correct perspective: They cast shadows, hide and are hidden by objects, and at times cast reflections into mirrors.
> They are perceived by both hearing and touch on occasion.

They may show details of appearance which are unrecognized by their observers and, in fact, by any person alive, and yet these details, upon investigation, may prove to be correct.

They are witnessed by two or more witnesses at the same time in a large percentage of cases listed.

Professor Hart also pointed out that phantasms possess many characteristics which show that they are only partially objective in their nature.

They appear and disappear mysteriously, are on occasion self-luminous and are seen, at times, by one or more witnesses, and yet other persons present may not be able to see them. This characteristic may also be explained by a differing ability within various people to perceive apparitions. [This principle I believe to be an absolute fact.]

Apparitions quite often "walk" through walls, etc.

They frequently are elevated from the ground and sometimes "float" up from floor or ground levels.

Their communications have been received by a telepathic process.

Animals have been known to sense the presence of phantoms or activity suggestive of their presence. This fact has been commented upon many times. The famed scientist Alfred Wallace argued in his *Miracles and Modern Spiritualism* that the perception of phantoms by animals shows that they are, at least in some cases, objective in their nature, and that telepathic theories attempting to explain this phenomenon are completely inadequate. He refers to the oft-quoted account by General Barter in which he describes his encounter with an amazingly complex apparitional display and his dog's reactions to the phantasmic activity (*Proceedings*: S.P.R., Part VI, p. 151), the reactions of dogs at Epworth Parsonage, the behavior of dogs at the Tedworth disturbance, the fear of a dog when it saw an apparition of a "white lady" described in a case contributed by Dr. Hodgson in *The Arena*, September, 1890, etc.

In this general discussion, Wallace mentions a case (*Proceedings*: S.P.R., Part VI) which included wailing noises heard on one occasion, which so frightened a bulldog that it pushed its nose into a stack of firewood and remained there trembling. On another occasion, an "awful howling" was heard, which was followed by the sound of shrieks. Three dogs were seen to cower in abject fear, and one of them retreated under a bed. When it was pulled out, it was discovered to be trembling. I can well sympathize with the state of the dogs in this haunted rectory in Staffordshire.

Wallace notes that Mrs. Sidgwick commented that, if natural causes were not responsible for the strange sounds, then the theory of collective hallucination via telepathy could be applied. Wallace wrote that it first must be shown that natural sounds can disturb dogs in such a drastic and peculiar fashion and it must also be proven that collective hallucinations can be received by one's pets—much less the question if such presumed hallucinations even exist. The famed scientist did not, clearly, favor Mrs. Sidgwick's evasions of what he considered the obvious fact that, because of the dog's reactions to the sounds, they must therefore be considered objective in their nature. I agree.

What can be called the reign of Mrs. Sidgwick at the Society for Psychical Research lasted for many years. She obviously was a woman of great intellect and was extremely active in psychical research—of this there is no doubt. However, she was remarkably opinionated, and what she did not favor she attempted to banish from the psychical horizons. The physical phenomena of psychism were on her index and she fought the idea that they existed tooth and nail. But, with people who cannot abide something which disturbs their accustomed way of thinking, clear and unmuddied reasoning soon vanishes. Apparitions which possessed some degree of objectivity and which were not hallucinatory were also on her list of phenomena which were not socially acceptable. But, unfortunately for the clearness of her judgment, they also existed.

Dr. Isaac K. Funk repeated Wallace's discussion in *The Widow's Mite* and commented favorably on the scientist's reasoning. Dr. Funk, I must say, was an investigator who maintained great independence of action and thought, was an expert in mediumistic fraud, and witnessed many genuine psychical cases featuring physical phenomena. He is, in large part, forgotten today.

Another investigator of the same period—one might almost say of the same circle—was Dr. Minot Savage, who contributed an animal percipient case in his *Can Telepathy Explain?* (G. P. Putnam's Sons, 1903, pp. 46–48). Dr. Savage did not give names and verifying material in his book, but such material was always available to qualified researchers, and his reputation was such that his writings were accepted as factual and of great value.

A young lady, a parishioner of Dr. Savage, while seated at her piano saw her dog, who was resting nearby, suddenly rise; saw the hair stand up on his back and heard him growl. She realized that he was gazing away from her. Looking to see what had alarmed him, she saw three shadowy figures in a front room. One figure was probably recognized before all three faded from sight. Her pet became so badly frightened that he took refuge under a couch.

It would be hard indeed to escape the conclusion that these phantoms possessed some degree of "visual objectivity" in that they were seen by two witnesses—one an animal. To be exact, the fact that her pet had seen the apparitions is a very valuable touch, particularly when it is remembered that he had seen the phantasmic figures first. Unfortunately, her pet did not have the foresight to provide a detailed, signed statement attesting to the facts for the edification of future researchers. A most regrettable oversight indeed!

Another case related to the two cases outlined above is included in the *Proceedings*: S.P.R., Vol. V, p. 453, and describes an experience which happened to an artist, Mr. Goodall, while he was visiting a village near Naples. Mr. Goodall was sitting on a donkey when it suddenly fell to its knees, throwing the narrator to the ground.

About the third or fourth night of his stay he awakened during the night and heard himself saying that he knew his daughter, May, had died. He then heard a voice, apparently not his own, say that his youngest son, not his daughter, had died.

Investigation revealed that the accident with the donkey, as best as could be judged, occurred at the same time as did the death of the writer's child. He believed that the donkey could have seen an apparition of the child.

A case of interest is given in Flammarion's *The Unknown* (Case CXXX). One morning a woman doctor heard a series of taps sounding on her bed. She happened to look at her cat, who was lying on the bed. His fur was standing erect with fear and she heard him growling. (Yes, cats do growl. I speak from experience.) The doctor became alarmed when she heard her bedroom door lightly shaken and, in fear, she shut her eyes. Later, she received word of the death of a friend.

The reaction of her cat certainly suggests the presence of an "invisible" phantom, and I find this explanation far more adequate than to assume that her cat first had received a telepathic impression of a death before further phenomena occurred.

In *Phantasms of the Living*, Case 350 includes a dog who howled nearly simultaneously with the sighting of a phantom. Mrs. Margaret Willink was told by her nurse that she and other employees had been disturbed by the howling of a dog who was chained outside the house. They had looked up from their occupations and seen a "ghostly face," which they recognized as that of a Mrs. Robinson who lived close-by in the village. One of the witnesses later was shown a photographic album in which she saw a photograph that was identical to the mysterious face which had appeared at the kitchen window. Mrs. Robinson had died within twelve hours of the appearance of her ghost. Another witness recognized the apparition as Mrs. Robinson immediately.

There seems little reason to doubt that the howling of the dog represented an awareness and probable sighting of the apparition, and as such added another "witness" to the sighting.

One last case involving an animal percipient will be very briefly outlined. It is included in *Death and Its Mystery: After Death* (Letter 4479). Perhaps the first thing to be mentioned is that the percipient and her grandmother, whose phantom she saw, had an understanding that the grandmother, after death, would contact her in any way she could. A phantom identical to the grandmother in appearance was seen by the narrator when she was in bed, and blew her a kiss. A little dog who was in the room jumped up on the bed howling just before the phantom was seen. The following morning confirmation of the grandmother's death was received by telegram.

I believe that it is not necessary to include any more examples of this type of case for illustrative purposes. The few given provide typical cases of animal percipience of phantoms and are similar to many others that can be found in parapsychological literature which offer data aiding those who find the various telepathic theories inadequate.

It has often been said, that if apparitions do exist and are objective in some degree, why have they not been photographed? In some ways, this question is rather naïve, but, as with other such comments, it possesses enough merit to warrant an answer.

The most obvious is simply that apparitions are in the main spontaneous in nature and are thoroughly unpredictable. One could never be prepared to snap their picture with a ready camera, even in cases of hauntings where the presence of apparitions is reported.

Further, apparitions are of varying degrees of objectivity. One person might see a phantom and yet another person standing close-by might be completely unable to perceive it. In a group which collectively sees a phantom, the would-be photographer might be the one unfortunate who was unable to see the apparition. Many difficulties, then, stand in the way of photographing apparitions.

However, in spite of such complications, cases do exist

where apparitions have been successfully photographed. To give a case in point, a prime case, two men were accidentally killed by gasoline fumes when sailing on the *S.S. Watertown*, which was a gasoline tanker bound for the Panama Canal from San Pedro, California. They were buried at sea on December 4, 1924, off the Mexican coast in 1,400 feet of water.

Close to dusk the next day, a ship's officer first saw the heads of the two dead men in the sea. These phantasmic heads were seen from the position where their bodies had been dropped into the ocean.

The faces were seen usually late of day and apparently floated close to each other. They were seen by almost the entire crew of the vessel.

When the ship passed through the Panama Canal into the Atlantic Ocean, the apparitional heads ceased to be seen. After the *Watertown* made port and started on her return voyage, the heads were seen repeatedly. A camera had been brought on board in the hope that the mysterious phantoms could be photographed. The captain managed to take six pictures of the heads and, when the films were developed and printed, it was discovered that five resulted in mundane pictures of waves, but a sixth revealed two faces apparently floating in the sea. The negative and print were examined on request of Mr. James S. Patton, an official of the shipping company which owned the *Watertown*. The photographic material was studied by the photographic department of the Burns Detective Agency, and the conclusion was reached that no sign of fraudulent manipulation could be found. The negative was originally developed by a commercial photographer.

On the *Watertown*'s third voyage after the men's death, the heads were seen a few more times, and that was the end of the remarkable sightings.

Hereward Carrington became interested in this strange case, studied it, and included an account of it in *The Invisible World* (The Beechhurst Press, 1946, pp. 127–32). A very, very brief version of the case is given in *Forgotten Mysteries* (Cloud, n.d.) by R. Dewitt Miller. Another far more complete description of the case is given by Vincent Gaddis in his excellent work devoted to mysteries of the sea, both natural and unnatural, entitled *Invisible Horizons* (Chilton Books, 1965).

The case, in spite of a certain amount of brevity, is an extremely important one and presents worthy evidence for the reality of photographing phantoms. Its bearing on the nature of apparitions is of great significance, and it demonstrates very dramatically that phantoms are definitely objective in that they reflect light, are collectively observed, represent the dead, and can be photographed—a splendid testimony to their physical reality.

Collectively viewed phantasms are so very well known that I will include only brief mention of such cases, but, to insure that this work is complete, a few examples must be incorporated. Earlier in this chapter examples of collectively perceived apparitions were given, not only to illustrate the fact that group sightings render the telepathic theories improbable, but that they are seen according to correct perspective and parallax by more than one witness at the same time. This fact alone demonstrates the total inappropriateness of telepathic explanations.

A very good example of a collectively viewed phantasm is

the Bettany case, included in that most useful well of apparitional data, *Phantasms of the Living* (Case 323). Mr. Bettany wrote in 1884 that he had seen a phantom woman dressed in a hood and black cloak crouching in his bedroom. He watched the figure "stealthily" progress from a door in the bedroom to a wardrobe cabinet by the same wall. When it reached the cabinet, it instantly vanished. Mr. Bettany noticed that no light was illuminating the bedroom and, when the phantom vanished, the room was left in darkness. He also mentioned that the bedroom door was locked and consequently no one could have normally entered the room.

Mrs. Bettany wrote that she awakened to find her husband staring at the apparition, which she also saw by the wardrobe. She commented that at first she thought the intruder was a real person but, when it disappeared mysteriously and it was realized later that the bedroom door was locked, all such thoughts were abandoned. She also wrote that the following day her child had told her nurse that she had seen the figure of an old woman in her room, but the nurse did not see the figure.

Cases of collectively perceived apparitions exist in large number—so large, in fact, that Tyrrell pointed out in 1953 that he had studied 130 such examples and had no doubt that there were many more. Professor Hart notes in "Six Theories about Apparitions" that in 156 cases involving phantoms, 46 featured other individuals placed so that during the appearances they would have seen the apparitions if they had been real persons. It is noted that 26 of these, or 56 percent, were witnessed collectively.

A particularly interesting case from *Phantasms of the Living* (Case 317) was described by two witnesses, Miss Violet and Miss Sidney Montgomery. Both witnesses were known to Sir William Barrett, to whom they originally reported the case.

The two sisters were driving home in a horse-drawn cart about 4:00 o'clock in the afternoon when above a hedge they saw a phantasmic figure of a woman floating. The strange figure was dressed in white, and floated about ten feet above the ground level in a "leaning" position. The phantom floated over the hedge and out over a field, and finally disappeared. The sisters believed that they watched the ghostly figure for perhaps two minutes. Their horse became so frightened that it suddenly halted and trembled in fear.

Another witness, a boy in the cart, also saw the phantom. Hence, it can really be said that four witnesses saw the apparition.

This case also provides a good example of an animal percipient, which certainly indicates that the apparitional figure possessed some degree of objectivity.

"Contagious telepathy" theorized by Edmund Gurney to explain collective sightings falls completely to pieces when confronted by complex cases such as this. As noted earlier in this chapter, Myers pointed out to Gurney that no evidence exists which shows that normal nonpsychic hallucinations are telepathically transmitted. At any rate, Gurney was not happy with his theory and undoubtedly realized that it involved far more complexities than did an explanation based on straight fact: namely, that when two or more witnesses claimed they saw an apparition, that is exactly what happened.

It was postulated by the earlier researchers that apparitions were not only completely nonobjective, but were merely the result of some order of telepathic transmission resulting in a hallucination of one or more senses. If one felt a touch, as did Mrs. Coote, who saw the figure of her sister-in-law bend over her, dressed in a nightdress, and wrote that the phantom definitely touched her, such an experience was labeled a tactile hallucination.

The percipient's aunt, living in an entirely different community, also saw the phantasmic figure at about the same time. She said that the figure apparently first appeared as a light in her bedroom and that the phantom was so distinct that she was able to see the pattern of the needlework on its nightdress.

This case originally appeared as No. 314 in *Phantasms of the Living.*

The fact that the phantom was seen by two witnesses living far apart at about the same time does indicate, at first glance, a telepathic origin for the phenomenon. But a counterexplanation can be given. There is no reason that a semiobjective apparition of the dead or dying sister-in-law could not have appeared to both witnesses. In such cases, where the possibility exists that the agent projected a phantom while dying, "astral projection" is definitely implied. It will be noticed by the reader of *Phantasms of the Living*, for example, that, in many cases in which apparitional figures were seen or felt, the agent was in all probability dying at the time of the apparitional appearance. Cases of this order will be discussed in the chapter devoted to "astral projection."

Many, many cases exist which present evidence showing that the phantoms seen were definitely semiobjective in certain ways. Physical objects have been moved or influenced, and a theory postulating hallucinatory origins cannot properly explain away the evidence for some degree of physical reality.

The often-mentioned phantom witnessed by the Reverend W. G. Gwynne and his wife (*Phantasms of the Living*, Vol. 11, pp. 202-3) illustrates this point perfectly. They saw a draped apparitional figure pass through their bedroom one night, and the Reverend Gwynne thought it pointed to their night light. At the same time while his wife held his arm, the light was extinguished when the phantom put its hand over it. So assured was the Reverend Gwynne that the intruding figure was real and, in fact, a servant, that he leapt from his bed and made a search of the room. No one could be found.

In this case, physical reality is argued not only by the fact that the phantom was capable of extinguishing a light, an argument quite unanswerable, but was collectively seen as well. With such an example even Mr. Tyrrell's "stage carpenter" would wear thin.

This theory, of course, insists that not only is a telepathic mechanism involved but that the viewer's subconscious enters into the picture as well as the subconscious mind of the sender, and as a result a phantom (which may include sounds and touches) is built up by everyone involved.

Such a theory is so all-inclusive that it would be practically impossible to advance any evidence, no matter how conclusive, for the objectivity of an apparition. If there were ninety-five witnesses who saw a phantom enter a room and calmly knock over a vase, all, according to Tyrrell's theory, had entered into an infernally complicated mental process which had constructed a mass hallucination of all the senses. The broken vase might be a bit awkward but it could, I am sure, be explained away by a determined Tyrrellite.

Obviously, such a theory, after a certain point is reached, becomes ridiculous and so weighty with complications and additions that it loses all claims to rationality. In fact, it almost can be identified with extreme solipsism. By the same token, if a living person sees another living person, or if several living people see another person, they are clearly creating a complex hallucination à la Tyrrell, and I defy anyone to disprove it by his rules of the game. In other words, no one could prove that anyone else existed other than as a hallucination instigated by another person. I do think it is time to draw down the curtain mercifully on this general hypothesis.

From *Phantasms of the Living* (Case 214) comes a case contributed by Mr. S. J. Masters, which offers a phantom with a definite objective characteristic. Mr. Masters was preparing for bed and was standing close to the open door of another bedroom when he saw a woman's figure in the doorway. He stated that he was able to see the phantom's eyes and its general features clearly. He wrote that he stood amazed for about twenty seconds staring at the figure. When his mother called to him, the figure vanished. The death of a friend coincided closely to the appearance of the apparition. Mr. Masters noticed particularly that the figure intercepted a light which he held in his hand shadowing a nearby wall.

In *Haunted Houses* (D. Appleton & Co., 1924, pp. 252–53) by Professor Flammarion, a case is given which describes how Mlle. X. from her bed (which was in a building considered to be haunted) saw the bed curtains disturbed. She picked up a lamp to see what was occurring and saw a phantasmic hand pass over the curtains and then disappear. In spite of the disappearance of the hand, the curtains still continued to be shaken.

This example is especially interesting because it shows clearly the frequently encountered mixture of apparent subjectivity and objectivity with psychical phenomena. In such a case it can be theorized that, in spite of the fact that the hand disappeared from view, it was still present in physical though invisible form.

This suggestion is borne out with observations of experimental séance phenomena. Touches were, of course, commonly felt during séances which presented genuine physical effects produced by noted mediums such as Kathleen Goligher and Eusapia Palladino. Many of these touches were produced by an unseen cause but, in spite of the invisibility of the "toucher," the physical reality of the touches was beyond dispute.

I have myself been touched in experimental séances on occasion by a very objective "toucher," which I am sure was completely invisible. One example, for instance, provided a positive, strong touch made by a finger which was strangely far warmer than would have been a touch by a living finger. A fellow experimenter encountered this same odd characteristic.

My wife, Marjorie, was touched during a sitting which was held in dim light. However, there was sufficient light to see that nothing physical had touched her, and again we have an invisible but objective "toucher."

The observations of Dr. W. J. Crawford are particularly valuable when the mechanisms of "touching" and, in fact, the entire field of telekinesis are considered. For example, Dr. Crawford requested the "operators" to extend a "rod," an "ectoplasmic" extension from the medium's body (Kathleen Goligher) to a dish filled with clay. In this manner he was able to take the imprint of the contacting surface and study the characteristics of these "rods." Many times this procedure was conducted in red light, and the experimenter was able to watch the entire process take place. However, in spite of the fact that perfectly concrete impressions were taken, the psychic extensions were invisible. The relationship of Dr. Crawford's observations and experiments to the nature of apparitions, particularly when objects are influenced by apparitional forms, is clearly seen.

It should be added that in 1921 Dr. E. E. Fournier D'Albe had twenty sittings with Kathleen Goligher and arrived at a negative verdict regarding the phenomena he witnessed with her. However, he wrote in a "formal" statement that he did see inexplicable phenomena, including the mysterious removal of a bottle stopper made of porcelain from a jar containing mercury. He was unable to back up his negative opinion with any provable incidents involving fraud, and, as Mr. Carrington remarked in *The Story of Psychic Science*, even those of the most skeptical turn of mind did not support his reports. I think, then, that D'Albe's speculations can be ignored for lack of concrete evidence. As such, they are not entitled to serious consideration.

I well remember that Hereward Carrington told me that he did think that real phenomena were observed by Dr. Crawford with the Golighers, and this statement is of great significance when it is remembered that Carrington was undoubtedly *the* great authority on mediumistic fraud and authored the famous text on that subject entitled *The Physical Phenomena of Spiritualism.*

In 1920, F. W. Warrick sat with Miss Goligher. The medium was then married and, though she was adverse to giving further sittings, her husband, Mr. Donaldson, prevailed upon her to give a number of special séances. She sat with Mr. F. M. Stephenson in 1933 for a number of sittings, and Mr. Warrick attended one test. Another sitting was held in April, 1935, and still another was held in October of the same year. Her husband took infrared photographs, and Mr. Stephenson also attended this experiment. The last sittings which are known to me were two tests held in 1936. They also were attended by Stephenson, Warrick, and the medium's husband.

I have discussed the case of Kathleen Goligher to some slight extent because of the obvious application of Dr. Crawford's discoveries to the study of apparitions, and because I consider that the medium has been shamefully neglected in contemporary thought.

From *Phantasms of the Living*, Vol. 1, 532, a case is given which tells how the percipient, Miss J. S., saw an apparition of her cousin, whom she believed to be alive at the time. The apparition entered through a door which "he" had just opened and pressed his hand into his chest. The viewer believed that "he" was indicating that he was not cold but that his lungs pained him and he could not speak.

The doctor walked into the room while Miss S. was still speaking to the apparition, which was only visible to her, and asked to whom she was talking. When he was told, he was shocked and told Miss S. that her cousin had been dead for half an hour.

The narrator was particularly impressed by the fact that she had heard the turning of the doorknob and had seen the door open. In a case of this type, objectivity of the phantom is strongly argued by circumstances.

Phantoms which perform acts resulting in definite physical effects do occur in hauntings. For example, during the Willington Mill Haunting described in the *Journal*: S.P.R., Vol. V, and more conveniently in *Poltergeist over England* (Country Life Ltd., 1945) by Harry Price, an apparition was seen to take up a candle snuffer and extinguish a light. There is no dearth of reports of physical acts in conjunction with apparitional activity in haunting cases, but this subject will be dealt with in a separate chapter.

With the phenomenon of astral projection, objective phenomena are occasionally encountered. For example, Dr. Robert Crookall in *The Study and Practice of Astral Projection* (Case 100) includes a case wherein a "projector" found herself in the home of her cousin. She saw a friend sleeping and pulled at her arm to awaken her. Her friend roused from her sleep, and clearly saw the apparitional form of the projector. Later the friend stated that she had felt her arm pulled and saw the phantasmic form of the projector.

Again, the entire phenomena of astral projection furnish evidence that apparitional activity with this effect and objective manifestations are on occasion found together. However, this subject will also be dealt with later on.

CHAPTER THREE

NONPHYSICAL

PHANTOMS

THE FACT that there are apparitions independent of the viewer that possess some physical characteristics and are nontelepathic in origin in no way denies the existence of phantoms which clearly are of subjective origin. A quick survey of phantoms soon reveals a large order which have been telepathically induced. Unfortunately, at the present, there are no statistics available which would determine definitely the percentage of each class.

One of the most obvious types of apparition which apparently is completely nonobjective is that combining horses and riders, in which the rider was known to have been dead and the animal involved was alive at the time of the appearance of the apparition. A few examples will be given by way of illustration.

Flammarion gives, in *Death and Its Mystery: At the Moment of Death* (pp. 351–52), a case which provides a composite phantom of this nature. Monsieur and Madame Pouzolz were leaning on a balcony of their house and heard a clock strike three. A few minutes passed and they saw a horseman in the distance riding toward them. As the horse and rider drew near, they saw that the rider was their father. As they watched, he stopped and dismounted by a gate. The young people, fully expecting to meet their father, walked from the balcony. They went outside but saw no one. Puzzled, they went completely around the house, again found no one, and still again circled the house, each going a different way. The mystery was tragically solved when news was received of their father's sudden death at three o'clock.

The composite phantom clearly did not reflect reality, because both horse and rider were not actually close to the house. It is not said in the original account whether the phantom rider had died while mounted on his horse, but the way the account read leads me to believe that such was not the case.

Flammarion preferred to classify this apparition as an example of a telepathic transmission—albeit a complex one subject to the difficulties which Gurney encountered with his telepathic "infection" theory. It can also be postulated that the phantom was actually independent of its viewers and represented the thoughts of the dead man after death. In other words, the surviving spirit of the horseman, dazed in the immediate after-death period, mentally dwelt upon his ride to his home, and this thought was telepathically received by his family, and then cast, via the subconscious, into the form of visual hallucination or apparition.

It can, of course, be theorized that the phantoms were simply the result of a telepathic transmission by the dying man. But this suggestion, in many cases, encounters the difficulty that the death of the agent or sender occurred so fast that it is hard to see how sufficient mental activity, if any, was present to create a telepathic transmission. In certain examples, this problem constitutes a most formidable argument against the belief that the agent "sent" out a telepathic "broadcast."

However, it has been suggested by a number of contemporary parapsychologists that a telepathic "field" is constantly present between individuals, thus rendering it unnecessary for an agent to directly transmit a telepathic message. In other words, the receiver is also "in touch" with the agent, knows when an accident occurs, and by means of an unconscious process then proceeds to conjure up an evidential apparition. This theory, plus additional features, is frequently used to avoid the survival hypothesis and, to my mind, represents an obvious evasion. More of this later.

Case 223 from *Phantasms of the Living* offers an account which tells how the narrator, while attending a concert, felt a mysterious cold sensation, and then saw her uncle appearing as though he was lying on a bed dying. She remarked that the "vision" seemed very real and "solid-looking" but, in spite of its realistic appearance, she could still see the orchestra behind the phantom. Soon after this incident she received a letter which informed her that her uncle had died.

Clearly, an apparition of this type is not objective in that a phantom bed composed of semi-matter and occupying space was not present. A telepathic process is implied.

Respecting this entire problem of objective versus nonobjective apparitions, Dr. Raynor Johnson in *Psychical Research* has written in Chapter 7, "Apparitions and Hauntings," that he favors the theory that phantoms range from the "Tyrrell" type, completely subjective in nature, to those semiobjective in their construction, to completely objective, solid materializations such as Dr. Geley, Sir William Crookes, Harry Price, and others encountered during their investigations. I most definitely agree with this view and believe that the "schematic" advanced by Dr. Robert Crookall (the "vehicle of vitality," etc.) provides the theoretical mechanisms of such phenomena.

At this point, I believe it is wise to outline very briefly Dr. Crookall's theory of the "vehicle of vitality" and its part in paranormal phenomena. On the basis of evidence resulting from his vast survey and analysis of mediumistic communications, the phenomena of astral projection, the physical phenomena of psychism, deathbed cases, etc., he believes that the evidence is conclusive to postulate an "etheric double," the "vehicle of vitality," which is composed of ectoplasmic material, semiphysical in nature, which occupies a halfway position between the physical world in which we live and the psychical state into which we pass after death. The "vehicle of vitality" is the ectoplasmic substance which, when directed, causes the physical phenomena found in the séance room, such as raps, telekinesis, and spontaneous manifestations, but in itself has no consciousness. After death, the "soul body" parts from the enshrouding vehicle of vitality and, thus freed, continues its existence fully aware in its new realm. The ectoplasmic material immediately after death and in a certain category of astral projection can cloud the consciousness, creating a dreamlike and confused mental state. Mediums who produce physical effects possess a loose "vehicle" which, being semiobjective, creates the various phenomena of the séance room.

According to this theory, a newly dead person, whose death was caused by unnatural means such as an accident, is shrouded by an enveloping ectoplasmic sheath—the vehicle of vitality—which is ideoplastic in nature. In other words, this substance is molded by thought and can assume various forms. Therefore, a person who has died by accident, or one who has died quite young, is for a certain period in a dazed, dreamlike state, and can produce an apparitional picture, a persona of himself which reflects his thoughts. Consequently, a person who has died by drowning might create an apparitional form which gives the appearance of accompanying dripping water.

According to this theoretical mechanism, many apparitional oddities which have apparently represented a purely telepathic process might well be explained.

Again from Flammarion, in his *The Unknown* (p. 96), a case is offered in which the narrator told how his uncle observed his brother-in-law one morning riding toward him on horseback. The uncle's wife was accordingly told that the horseman would soon arrive, but strangely the rider was not seen again. Afterward news was received which told that the brother-in-law had suffered a stroke and had fallen from the mount he was riding.

There is no question in this case of the horse's dying at the same time as did its rider. Therefore, the horse and presumably its rider cannot have been an objective apparition reflecting literal fact; it could have been a visual hallucination resulting from a telepathic transmission. If one prefers, the "field theory" might be applied here, inasmuch as agent and percipients were in constant "touch" via the "psychical field" (if such exists) and then by this means a visual image was constructed. Personally, I am not overly taken with the field theory of telepathy and, at times, prefer the older and simpler hypothesis of telepathic transmission from agent to percipient. I do think, however, that in certain phenomena some type of paranormal field may possibly exist.

From the standpoint of a telepathic transmission from sender to receiver, there are several difficulties which bar a clear understanding of such cases. If, in this case, the apparition resulted from a telepathic transmission from the dying man, then why, it can be asked, did not the vision reflect the actual incident: the stroke and the fall from the horse? Why does the dying man create only a "picture" of himself riding a horse with no hint of his dying experience?

Various suggestions can be advanced to explain this seeming oddity. Perhaps the most obvious is that the rider simply was struck so swiftly by, in this last case, a stroke, or in other cases by physical injury, that he did not actually realize that death was upon him. The mind was filled with the thought, the desire to return home, or to fulfill whatever activity was being engaged in, and these last reasonably coherent thoughts were then perhaps transmitted and reconstructed via the subconscious into a visual phantom.

On the other hand, assuming that the individuals in such death incidents survived their physical demise—and, as I have mentioned, I am convinced that from all available evidence, survival is fact—then according to Dr. Crookall's theory they, due to accidental death or youthful death, were enshrouded by the mentally confusing "vehicle of vitality" or ectoplasmic material and very probably their immediate after-death thoughts reflected their last desires or acts: i.e., the desire to return home.

A source of possible confusion lies in the definition of the word "apparition." In the type of cases just discussed, there seems every reason to consider that, even though they originate from the dead or dying, they still are quite nonobjective in their nature and essentially differ little from a typical, spontaneous telepathic "flash." It is perhaps impossible to differentiate in many cases between subjective and objective character, and it is, to my mind, obvious that certain apparitions may possess both characteristics simultaneously.

Gardner Murphy, who apparently likes the idea that he might eventually find himself surviving death as much as cats like water, postulated (as have others) the theory that the percipient of such apparitions is the author of such visions, not the transmitter, according to previous theories. He has written that in cases of apparitions, the unconscious of the viewer who has received an original telepathic impulse, whatever its nature, may rummage wildly through all time—past, present, and future—to create a suitable phantom.

Well! With this speculation, in a race between the horse and the cart, the Murphian cart clearly won.

This theory and others like it, which can be lumped under that all-inclusive title, the super-ESP theory, can be used to explain away anything by the convinced nonsurvivalist. It can easily be equated with Deity, and in my opinion should be received with humor and some contempt.

With this theory, this utterly extravagant speculation, the old-fashioned devil theory has really been surpassed. As we know, the devil hypothesis insists that any and all psychical phenomena are the work of devils and hellishly designed to deceive mankind.

Oh, it is quite true that one cannot actually disprove the devil theory. If one desires, one can substitute green trolls or little fairies, and anything else one wishes, but it can easily be shown that such a concept is hopelessly extravagant, does not fill all known facts as does, for example, the survival theory, and for its acceptance really demands a most resolute credulity. Certainly the most naïve spiritualist never exceeded the near-cosmic claims of the super-ESP theory. It really seems to be constructed of the same elements as those in small children's arguments when one will say to another, "No matter what number you write, I can write a bigger one!" True, true, but how silly!

Gardner Murphy once advanced (against the theory that certain apparitions represent activity instigated by the dead) the suggestion that animal apparitions show that survival of death cannot be. His point was that our belief in survival of death springs from our artistic, intellectual, and moral abilities. Since animals do not possess any of these characteristics and yet animal apparitions do occur, apparitions do not constitute evidence for surviving spirits. His thought also implies that, due to the greatly lesser abilities of animals when compared to human beings, they too cannot survive death.

In my opinion, this argument is confused and in its parts is placed thoroughly backward. The sensible and obvious question that should be asked is: If human beings can survive death, why cannot animals do the same? From this point on, it becomes merely a question of evidence, not personal préjudice.

An example of an apparition which was clearly subjective in its nature is given in *Phantasms of the Living* (202), which provides what can be termed a classical example of a nonobjective vision or phantom.

A Miss S. left her house and was riding in a carriage when she saw a friend, Mrs. A., with one of her children riding toward her. As their carriages passed, Miss S. saw her friend in three-quarter view and was able to see the exact nature of her clothing: a sealskin coat and a particular bonnet. Miss S.

called out to her friend but received no answer. Two or three days after this incident Miss S. read in a newspaper the notice of her friend's death. It was discovered later that the apparition had appeared about two hours before Mrs. A.'s death, at a time when she was unconscious and dying.

The simplest solution of this curious apparition is to theorize a telepathic process, with or without a "paranormal field," according to the reader's taste. The apparition (it might be better to term it a hallucinatory vision) was obviously subjective in its nature, for not only was a child seen but a phantasmic coach as well.

The time element, of course, poses another problem—one which will be overlooked for the moment inasmuch as the purpose in including this interesting example is to present an apparition of an unarguable nonobjective order.

The apparition which appears to one person, yet is unseen by another close-by, is very common and is met frequently in parapsychological literature. Podmore lists a typical example in his *Apparitions and Thought Transference* (Chapter XI, No. 73). Miss Berta Hurly wrote that during part of the year 1886 she had frequently called upon a poor and ailing woman, Mrs. Evans, who enjoyed her visits. Miss Hurly had not visited her for a few days and after dinner, in the presence of her family, she saw an apparition of the sick woman pass through the room. The figure was so real that its clothing was recognized as to detail. Miss Hurly called out to the phantom and, when her mother asked her why she did this, she was told that a figure of a woman had just walked through the dining room. She was laughed at for her words, but she believed that the phantom was Mrs. Evans. The following morning it was discovered that, at about the time the figure had appeared, the sick woman had lapsed into unconsciousness. She died near the morning.

In this case, the simplest and most economical explanation is to assume that the dying woman "astrally projected" from her body to Miss Hurly, who had shown her kindness. It can, of course, be said that the apparition was the result of a telepathic process.

For the purposes of this chapter, however, it does offer an apparitional figure which was not seen by other members of the family and, therefore, can be placed in the category of nonobjective phenomena. It must be remembered, though, that this classification is very arbitrary indeed, and the very probable ability of certain people to sense paranormal phenomena more than others must be considered. This, I think, is a definite fact.

Apparitions have, then, been divided so far into two main categories: subjective phantoms seen only by the percipient, and objective or partially objective phantoms which are frequently seen collectively, and on occasion are seen according to correct perspective and, in certain cases, perform "physical" actions such as extinguishing lights, moving bed curtains, creating audible footsteps and rustling clothing as they walk. There is, then, no reasonable purpose to be gained in holding to the now obsolete belief that apparitions must all be subjective in their structure.

Interestingly, Schopenhauer, in spite of his denial that we can survive death, wrote that he believed that the dying are able to project an image of themselves to their absent friends, but that these projections are purely subjective in their nature.

An interesting case of a subjective apparition given by

Flammarion in *Death and Its Mystery: After Death*, Chapter 3, tells how a young boy in a hospital told his mother that he saw his father, who had died two years before. His mother told him that no one was there, but the child insisted that he saw his father. It is noted in the account that neither the boy's mother nor a nurse who was present could see any visible manifestation. The sick boy then said that his father was calling him and wished to take him with him. While still claiming that he could see and hear his dead father, the boy became unconscious and died "some days later." A volunteer nurse, a Mrs. Chambers, described the incident.

Using this example to illustrate such cases, it is very clear that, in such "meeting" episodes, definite intention is manifested in that the phantom represents a surviving spirit coming to help the dying person leave his physical body. Of course, other explanations can be offered, including the suggestion that the boy was simply hallucinating and imagined that his father was present. However, when this type of case is placed in the vast mosaic of psychism, the survivalistic theory becomes the simplest and most appropriate explanation.

With this case, another variety of "subjective" phantom is presented, and the title "subjective apparitions" clearly becomes a rather loose classification covering a number of types of cases. Of course, this is also the case with the classification of objective apparitions.

It is difficult to suggest a difference in mechanism between many subjective apparitions and crystal visions, hypnogogic visions, certain visions of distant scenes, and death scenes. However, these related phenomena will, for the purposes of this study, not be discussed.

In a later chapter a theory which has been advanced by Professor Hornell Hart to replace previous telepathic theories will be analyzed.

CHAPTER FOUR

ANIMAL

APPARITIONS

APPARITIONS are not in the least limited to human forms but have also appeared in the form of animals. The phantom of the dog, Mac, who had belonged to Marie Demler, reported in my previous work, *Animal Ghosts*,[1] falls into this category, though in this case it possessed characteristics which indicated that it was not an objective form but was a nonphysical apparition resulting from a "telepathic" process.

A most interesting instance of an animal apparition, strongly survivalistic in tone, is given in Eleanor Sidgwick's *Phantasms of the Living* (G 286). Two sisters were seated by a window during the day, when they both saw their cat Smokey cross their lawn in a most lifelike fashion. As the cat continued its walk, the sisters noticed that it limped, a very characteristic trait. One sister rushed out of the house and called to the cat, but it paid her no attention and passed through a shrub and out of sight.

A few minutes later, the cat was once again seen by one of the sisters and a friend, who were by the same window from which the cat had originally been sighted. A search was hurriedly made, but no trace of the animal could be found.

[1] In *Animal Ghosts*, University Books Inc., 1970, I have included a number of animal apparitions along with data which in my opinion demonstrate that animals do survive death.

62

Still later in the day the cat was seen inside the house and, believing it to be alive, a servant offered it a drink of milk, which it ignored.

Needless to say, the cat was actually dead and, to prove this point, the gardener exhumed her body from under a dahlia bush where she had been recently buried.

This is a well-known case which provided an animal apparition. Immediately following the account is a note stating that a very similar occurrence is given in a S.P.R.: *Proceedings*. This other case offered a phantasmic white cat, which was observed by two witnesses.

The apparition of Smokey, on the face of it, does not fall into the subjective category. It was viewed collectively; it was not a crisis apparition, in that the phantom cat appeared some time after its death; it was totally unexpected; and its appearance was so very realistic that a servant attempted to feed it. Of course, this appearance of extreme reality in no way proves a phantom to be objective in nature, but this trait most certainly does not speak against objectivity.

Another very interesting example of the sighting of an animal apparition is printed in the *Proceedings*: S.P.R., Vol. XIV, and the account tells how a phantasmic little black and white terrier, Judy, ran through a room in the hotel where the narrator, Mrs. Mary Bagot, was staying. Mrs. Bagot was amazed to see her dog, because she had not brought her pet with her, and, being surprised, called the dog's name out loud. She later described to her daughter what she had experienced. Within a few days a letter arrived telling of her pet's death. Unfortunately, she could not remember the exact date the incident occurred but she said she thought Judy had died on the same day that she had seen the apparition.

An apparition of this order can be considered the result of a telepathic transmission from the dog itself. Much evidence indicates that animal telepathy does exist. On the other hand, it may be considered that someone with the dog telepathically transmitted the impulse received by Mrs. Bagot, which was then modified into a visual hallucinatory phantom that ran across the hotel room. By the same token, it can be equally well theorized that an actual, objective apparitional dog was seen. In cases of this type I fail to see how any clear-cut decision can be reached, but the survival theory explains such an incident perfectly.

The "Tweedale Haunting" furnishes animal apparitions of a most interesting order and, in a number of sightings, they clearly possessed some degree of objectivity. This most remarkable "haunting" which, in certain ways, should really not be placed in this category of phenomena, will be treated further in Chapter Nine. For the moment I will only refer to certain animal apparitions which are mentioned in the Reverend Tweedale's books, *Man's Survival After Death* and *News from the Next World.*

Cat apparitions were frequently seen after the pathetic death of "Willie" and her three little kittens. A phantom representing this family pet was seen on numerous occasions. "Willie" was missed during a wintery March day and could not be found. The Reverend Tweedale on June 17, 1932, found her body with her three dead kittens in a seldom-visited part of his gardens, where she had attempted to nurse them while dying of exposure. She and her little family were buried in a grave under the chestnut tree where they had tragically died, and the words "Willie Faithful" were carved into the tree's trunk by the Reverend Tweedale.

Some time later the Reverend Tweedale, when returning from church, stopped at the grave and very softly spoke aloud. Referring to her death, he expressed the wish that she gain a reward in the next world. He did not tell his family what he had done and, of course, was alone when he wished "Willie" well.

One year from the time she was missed (which was March 7, 1933) and three days after the Reverend Tweedale had spoken over her grave, his daughter, Dorothy, saw an apparition of "Willie" in the house. As she watched the phantasmic cat, it walked for a yard and then disappeared from sight.

At this time, the Tweedales had another cat, which was sleeping on a chair at the time of this sighting. On March 15th, the Reverend Tweedale's daughter, Sylvia, walking through a passage near the kitchen, also saw the apparitional "Willie," who walked a short distance and again spontaneously disappeared. The other cat, during this incident, was sleeping in another room.

On March 17th, the Reverend Tweedale was seated in a chair, when he saw "Willie" jump on his chair and then to a couch nearby. As he watched, the phantom apparently dissolved into the air. His daughter, Dorothy, saw the apparition at the same time, which, of course, provided a collective sighting. Again, their living cat was seen, undisturbed, sleeping on a chair during this sighting.

On April 30th, his daughter, Dorothy, saw "Willie" sitting on the floor and in full view suddenly disappear.

His daughter, Marjorie, on May 1st saw the apparitional cat, and on August 6th Dorothy again sighted "Willie" walking and subsequently disappearing in the usual fashion. In this case only the forepart of her body could be seen clearly. The rest was shaded into an indistinct blur.

The number of sightings plus the collective sighting of the Reverend Tweedale and his daughter, Dorothy, definitely argue for a degree of objectivity.

The "Tweedale Haunting" began in November, 1910, when phantoms were seen and paranormal voices heard. An apparitional dog which represented a pet which had belonged to a dead aunt, Leah Coates, was seen quite a number of times and was identified in a most evidential manner.

The first sighting of this phantasmal dog occurred on January 18, 1911, when Mrs. Tweedale and three daughters saw an apparitional dog, white in color, run up a flight of stairs to a bedroom and under a bed. Later that day a servant reported that the phantom dog had walked into a bedroom, and on another occasion Mrs. Tweedale said that, when she was carrying a burner and lamp glass, the ghostly animal jumped and dashed them from her hand. The glass was broken and the wall was spattered with flying oil.

One very important observation was made by Mrs. Tweedale when on January 27th and February 2, 1911, she saw the phantasmic dog and noted that it was a terrier, that it shivered noticeably, that its hair was extremely short so that its skin could be seen through it, and that it had a black oval spot on its back.

The Reverend Tweedale observed that his wife's report of the dog's appearance was important because of its evidential nature. Mrs. Tweedale had never seen the dog when it was alive, its image was not on any photograph, and the children and the servants had never seen it. It was, in life, very short haired and it did markedly shiver with excitement. It did have a black spot on its back and it was a terrier. The dog had belonged to the Reverend Tweedale's aunt, Leah Coates, who had died on August 13, 1905, and whose phantom also manifested repeatedly after 1910.

Mrs. Tweedale, on March 5th, talked to the paranormal voice which spoke for the dead aunt, and, after this curious discussion had ended, the phantom dog raced down a flight of stairs and playfully leaped at a gong, which caused it to ring. These actions of the ghostly creature were witnessed by both Mrs. Tweedale and a servant.

The phantasmic dog persisted in its appearance until August 22, 1915. That was approximately two years after the cessation of the appearance of the apparition of Leah Coates.

More details of this incredible "haunting" will be given later in the book, but for the moment I will rest content with noting that W. W. Baggally, the famed and skilled investigator who was associated with the Society for Psychical Research, and took part in the famous investigation of the great medium, Eusapia Palladino, along with Hereward Carrington and Everard Fielding, was impressed with the phenomena occurring with the Tweedales, studied it first hand, and was convinced that genuine paranormal effects took place.

Other animal apparitions were seen with the Tweedales, including numerous appearances of a black cat which was associated with communications presumably emanating from the great violin maker, Antonio Stradivari. To fully appreciate the remarkable phenomena which occurred with the Tweedales and to fully appreciate the extraordinary complexity of the case, one must read the Reverend Tweedale's *News from the Next World.*

The case mentioned at the beginning of this chapter citing

the appearance of the wet and dripping dog, Mac, who had belonged to the author, Marie C. Demler, which appeared to her when she was in a hospital, coincided with the dog's death by drowning. It furnishes a typical subjective case of animal apparition, since the phantom possessed no objective characteristics that were noticeable. It would have been interesting, of course, to see what might have occurred if another person had been present when the phantom entered the room.

A type of phantom which includes both humans and animals (and frequently vehicles as well) is what I termed, in *Animal Ghosts*, a composite apparition.

A typical example, with one exception, of a composite apparition is given in the *Journal*: S.P.R., October, 1893, which tells how, during a hunt, two sisters decided to leave, and their coachman drove them home. As they began their return all saw the girls' father riding a white horse, waving his hat, and noticed that the horse was extremely dirty. They attempted to meet him but could not find him. Later on, the father said that he had not waved to them and had not been in the area where they saw him. But during the hunt he had actually ridden a white horse.

The exception, of course, lies in the curious fact that the rider was not dead, hence the apparition was one of the living. "Ordinary" astral projection cannot be invoked, inasmuch as I doubt if anyone would seriously contend that both horse and rider simultaneously extruded a phantasmic double.

The case given in Flammarion's *Death and Its Mystery: At the Moment of Death*, and briefed in Chapter Three, which presented a phantasmic horse and rider seen by two witnesses, Monsieur and Madame Pouzolz, is a very typical example of this type of apparition. As mentioned, the two witnesses saw that the rider was their father and went to meet him. He did not arrive and, puzzled, they circled the house twice seeking him. Later news was received telling of his death at three o'clock, almost exactly the time that they saw the horse and rider.

Henry Holt includes a related example in his *On the Cosmic Relations*, Vol. I (pp. 271–72) an interesting example of such an apparition which seemingly was completely subjective in nature. At first view it seems unlikely that the vehicle seen had any objective characteristics, but, according to the text, the percipients heard the vehicle, a wagon, crash through the underbrush.

Dr. Rossiter Johnson and his secretary were riding in the countryside of Long Island during a moonlit night. As they were riding, a wagon pulled by a team of horses appeared in the field next to the road. A fence divided the road from the field and the phantasmic team walked close to the fence. There was no rider visible. The footsteps of the horses and the sound of the wagon wheels crashing through the border of weeds and brush certainly suggested some objective characteristics. Yet, at first sight, an objective wagon seems very unlikely. A truly difficult problem is posed by cases such as this. The apparition departed from the norm, to use that term, in that no human figure was included in the phantasm.

An example of a collectively viewed apparition which strongly suggests "astral projection" is given in the *Journal*: S.P.R., December, 1894, in the "Catalogue of Unprinted Cases."

Miss M. L. Pendered wrote that her mother and a friend

saw, lying on a hearth rug, a dog which had previously accompanied the friend's sister. It was subsequently discovered, when the sister returned, that the dog had almost drowned at the time his double was seen.

It can be easily theorized that a telepathic transmission from the sister who had the dog with her at the time of the accident produced the apparition. It can also be equally theorized that the dog, while "drowning," extruded an astral double exactly as does the human astral projector, and that the double was seen as a visual apparition. The phenomena of astral projection and its relationship to apparitions will be discussed later.

Other types of phantoms have been reported, and some were extraordinary in their complex and puzzling structure. For example, the well-known apparition seen by General Barter and described in *Proceedings*: S.P.R., Vol. V, offered hoofbeats of an oncoming horse, followed immediately by the composite apparition of a horse and rider and two accompanying grooms. The General saw that his two dogs, who were walking with him, crouched and whimpered in fear. He, with remarkable self-possession, addressed the phantom horseman, and the entire ghostly group halted. This action, I think, showed awareness on the part of the apparitional figures.

The horseman was later found to represent Lieutenant B., who had died and who was known to the General. Both General Barter and his wife heard the phantasmic footsteps on several succeeding occasions.

Frank Podmore investigated an exceedingly strange case which offered a carriage pulled by two horses with two men sitting on its box and a draped white figure, which seemed to be that of a woman. This entire group was completely phantasmic in nature, and both coach and horses left no telltale marks. Further, this eerie structure passed across the lawn in front of the home of the two witnesses, Major W. and his son. This interesting oddity will be found in Chapter XVIII of *Phantasms of the Living*.

Still another oddity (No. 202) is given in this same work and describes an apparitional structure composed of a woman and two children riding in an open carriage. The apparition was seen two hours before the death of the woman whom the phantom figure represented.

Obviously, animals figure frequently in phantasmic structures and may appear singly or even in groupings. There clearly are many varieties ranging from those possibly resulting from telepathic transmission to astral projections and phantoms of a survivalistic order.

D. J. West wrote in "The Investigation of Spontaneous Cases," *Proceedings*: S.P.R., Vol. XLVIII, Part 175 (p. 294), "For example, the 1935 talking mongoose[2] has its counterparts in the little animals seen in the Epworth Haunting and the Willington Mill manifestations of 1835–1847. The mongoose christened itself Jeff, whilst both the Willington Mill and the Epworth ghosts were familiarly referred to as Old Jeffrey. The mongoose, the Willington Ghost and the Ringcroft Ghost of 1695 were all described as making chuck-

---

[2] The case of a presumed abnormal "animal," which supposedly talked, is described in *The Haunting of Cashen's Gap* by Harry Price, and in *Haunted People: The Story of the Poltergeist Down the Centuries* by Hereward Carrington and Nandor Fodor. As Price points out, evidence in favor of the existence of this familiar-like creature is extremely weak. Fodor built an elaborate psychoanalytic edifice on speculation regarding the "mongoose" which, in my opinion, was much ado about nothing.

chucking noises, whilst Old Jeffrey of Epworth was reported to have gobbled like a 'turkey-cock.' "

West does not, obviously, care for the idea of small animal apparitions and wrote that a conformity in tradition with presumed paranormal phenomena does not indicate authenticity in the least.

He seems to have drawn his material regarding the strange chucking sounds heard with the Willington Mill case and the Ringcroft haunting, and the gobbling noises heard during the Epworth rectory disturbance from Price's observations of the similarity of sounds in the different cases described in *Poltergeist over England.*

When West wrote his paper, poltergeist cases were still regarded with little respect in many quarters, and consequently, I believe, his observations regarding animal apparitions were based on concepts prevailing at that time. More recently, however, numerous cases of poltergeist-hauntings have been studied firsthand by a number of researchers, including W. G. Roll, Professor Hans Bender, Dr. Gaither Pratt, and others. As recorded in previous books, I myself have been very fortunate in that I have personally witnessed haunting or poltergeist-haunting phenomena in two cases and have encountered several examples of spontaneous haunting effects.

With the growing acceptance of poltergeist-haunting phenomena, I believe that resistance to the thought, the possibility of animal apparitions, has probably lessened a great deal since the publication of West's paper.

CHAPTER FIVE

LUMINOUS

MANIFESTATIONS

AS IS thoroughly well known, death is frequently accompanied by many forms of psychical phenomena. The titles, for examples, of Professor Flammarion's classic trilogy, *Death and Its Mystery: Before Death*, *At the Moment of Death*, and *After Death*, indicate that such manifestations are grouped in the time period surrounding death. Apparitions are, of course, one of the most dramatic effects to be encountered at this time and have been seen in such number that they have become a part of traditional "occult" folklore. And, as so frequently is discovered, the belief largely reflects reality.

Outside the direct classification of apparitions, there is a very large body of evidence describing manifestations consisting of varied effects such as paranormal lights and rappings and poundings, some of which at first glance do not seem to fit too smoothly into an apparitional scheme. Then there are strange phenomena such as the splitting of table tops, glass objects breaking, stopping of clocks, explosive sounds, and many other psychical oddities.

Some very prominent phenomena during this crucial time period are the appearance of various types of luminous effects which range from apparitions which are self-luminous to mysterious illuminations of portions of rooms, "clouds of lights," and so forth.

Disks of lights are common, and phantoms frequently appear within circles of light. These phenomena have been encountered through the years and are quite well known. Interestingly, luminous disks, etc., have been observed during séances with mediums who produce physical manifestations such as paranormal voices, telekinetic effects, and raps. Disks of light have been seen with John Sloan, who was the remarkable voice medium observed by Arthur Findlay and Sir William Barrett.

During sittings with Mrs. Blanche Cooper, small blue-white circles of light were observed, and on occasion the outline of a human head, a hand, etc., were seen in luminous areas. S. G. Soal reported seeing these manifestations during the sittings which produced the famed but, to my mind, over-emphasized, Gordon Davis communications.

J. Malcolm Bird saw "luminous patches" with Evan Powell; and with Ada Bessinet, he saw lights, including one type which illuminated mysteriously appearing faces. The lights in themselves were not circular, however, but were shaped somewhat like a "large flower bud." Carrington as well as Professor Hyslop also witnessed lights with this medium.

At one sitting with Ada Bessinet, Professor Hyslop saw quite large lights and finally received objective evidence of their paranormality when messages were received written by means of the light's movements in the dark séance room. Hyslop wrote that these messages gave cross-references to messages received by other mediums.

Luminous effects have been seen with many mediums including Franek Kluski, D. D. Home, Mrs. Emily French, Indride Indridason, "Margery" Crandon, Frau Silbert, at least once with Valiantine, and other psychics. On one occasion Mr. Ceil Smith and I saw brilliant "sparks" of light, bluish-white in color underneath a chair in which Mr. Attila von Szalay, a friend and nonprofessional psychic, was sitting. The room was dimly lit but we could see that his hands, for example, were folded in his lap during this highly informal sitting.

All lights seen in the presence of mediums are not necessarily circular in shape but appear in various forms, and I suspect that in the present state of psychic science, any attempt to rigidly classify them would result in highly arbitrary categories.

Self-luminous apparitions have been seen as well as apparitions which have appeared inside luminous areas. So well known are the luminous phantoms that Lord Edward Bulwer-Lytton, who sat with D. D. Home, for example, incorporated the "legend" in his noted novel, *A Strange Story*. In this tale, Margrave, a fantastic figure possessing enormous charm, but no knowledge of good or evil, had the ability to project an "astral double." When he had accomplished this feat, however, he had no conscious memory of having done so. In Chapter XXXIX a description of Margrave's double is given: "And then, on the opposite side of the wall I beheld an unsubstantial likeness of a human form. Shadow I call it, but the word is not strictly correct for it was luminous, though with a pale shine. . . ."

In Chapter LXI Margrave is again seen in the following form: ". . . and reflected against the opposite wall, stood the hateful Scin Laeca [the astral double]. The Shadow was dimmer in its light than when before beheld, and the outline of the features was less distinct—still it was the unmistakable lemur, or image, of Margrave."

In this story, as in *Zanoni* and *The House and the Brain*, elements of genuine psychism are to be found in a literary ore of magic and generally extravagant occult lore. I must admit that by modern tastes Bulwer-Lytton's longer stories are slowly paced but, in spite of their leisurely gait, they still are quite interesting.

The concept of the "astral body," the human double, and out-of-the-body phenomena is now well accepted and has a long historical background. Bulwer-Lytton's Margrave with his luminous double is a literary representation of the astral body and its actions, and this general phenomenon and its relationship to apparitions will be more fully discussed in a later chapter.

In a study of luminous phenomena culled from cases found in the abridged version of *Phantasms of the Living* by Eleanor Sidgwick, and in the original by Gurney, Myers, and Podmore; in examples from *Death and Its Mystery* by Camille Flammarion; in *The Phenomena of Astral Projection* by Sylvan Muldoon and Hereward Carrington; and in *The Case for Astral Projection* by Muldoon, it is revealed that luminous phenomena occur in several forms. In the examples studied, out of twenty-six cases, thirteen represented paranormal activity instigated by living persons. Four of these cases provided phenomena which occurred before death. In other words, on the face of it, some apparitions were seen of people who at the time were living but who died shortly afterward.

On the basis of this very limited survey, it can be said that luminous phenomena, which are so very frequently associated with apparitional manifestations, seem equally divided between phenomena representing the living and those representing the dead.

A small number of cases were eliminated as they fell outside the pattern of "orthodox" psychical phenomena and therefore must be considered dubious or unusable at the present.

Certainly, one of the most famous cases of odd light effects associated with death and possible apparitional activity is the accumulation of observations and photographic evidence gained by Dr. Hippolyte Baraduc shortly after the turn of the century. Before describing briefly these curious photographs, it must first be admitted that Baraduc's general experiments and observations are subject to certain doubt. For example, in the June, 1971, issue of *Psychic*, J. Fraser Nicol offered a short history of Baraduc's experiments and stated that his work was frequently faulty in technique and his conclusions somewhat peculiar. Hereward Carrington remarked, in *The Problems of Psychical Research* (1921 edition), that, in spite of experimental lacks, the results obtained by the French experimenter are still thoroughly interesting and that further work along these lines should take place.

In the year 1907 André Baraduc, the son of Dr. Baraduc, died after he became ill with tuberculosis. Dr. Baraduc reported that six hours after his son died, his apparition appeared several times and communication took place between father and son. As Carrington wrote, such observations can only reflect personal conviction of a bereaved father, and, as such, possess no true value, evidentially speaking.

However, Dr. Baraduc, after nine hours had passed, photographed the body of his son and received very odd configurations on his plates. On the first plate was an amorphous, mistlike substance apparently issuing from the coffin. On another plate strange white treelike extrusions seemed to emerge from his son's body. This photograph as well as two others are reproduced in *Death: Its Causes and Phenomena* by Hereward Carrington and J. R. Meader. This same picture also appears in the issue of *Psychic* previously mentioned.

Dr. Baraduc's wife died six months after the death of André and, with what I consider admirable scientific courage, he began photographing her from the moment of her death. The first plate, which was immediately developed, revealed three large and roughly globular misty masses, apparently floating above his wife's body. Curious twisting streaks of light close to the misty forms also appeared on the plate. After fifteen minutes Dr. Baraduc took another photograph, and in this picture it was seen that two of the "globes" had merged into one.

Dr. Baraduc reported that as time passed one well-formed sphere floated over the body, separated itself, and floated into his bedroom, where he spoke to it. It finally disappeared. Dr. Baraduc insisted that for several days he saw globes of the same type about his house. No photographs were taken of these light masses. Obviously, it would have been almost impossible to have had a camera set up at the appropriate locations and times.

In spite of criticisms which have been leveled against his experimental techniques and his conclusions, his observations and the photographs match many accounts of phenomena which occur about the period of death, and as such are worthy of serious study.

For instance, in *The Phenomena of Astral Projection*, an account, originally given in Mrs. de Morgan's *From Matter to*

Spirit, is published which describes a white cloudlike mass which emerged from a dying person's body. Mrs. de Morgan and a friend witnessed this effect, and her friend described the happening in the following words: ". . . a white, nebulous light surging over the bedcovers. . . ." She also saw a small column which "radiated a luminosity. . . ."

Also in *The Phenomena of Astral Projection* will be found an account that appeared in a 1922 issue of *Light* which tells how a family of eight witnessed light phenomena at the death of their mother. At first they saw a small, white cloud form over her head and later saw the cloud lit up by a blue light as well as being "shot with blue scintillations." Still after, her head was crowned as it were by an aureole of yellowish color. These effects were noted as she was in the process of dying.

It will be seen, I am sure, that these two accounts, which actually represent a class of phenomena, reinforce the validity of Dr. Baraduc's observations and photographs.

A few illustrations of general luminous phenomena and luminous apparitions follow:

From Podmore's *Apparitions and Thought Transference* (Walter Scott, Ltd., 1894) two examples of apparitions which were seen in accompanying luminous areas provide good illustrations of this class of manifestation.

Case No. 71 includes a description by Miss L. Caldecott, who first saw a faint glow light up a dark corner of her room followed by the appearance of a friend within the lighted area. In this case the agent, the viewer's friend, was quite alive at the time and, in a letter to Miss Caldecott, wrote that during the evening when her apparition was seen, was wishing very strongly that she could have been with her friend.

It is clear, I am sure, that the apparition that was seen could well have been an extruded double, an astral projection.

In Case No. 72 a description is given by Dr. Carat, who told how he saw the end of his room lit up with a "silvery" illumination. He then saw his mother looking at him intently, and after a few seconds all manifestations ceased. In this example, Dr. Carat's mother, unknown to him, had become sick and died at approximately the same time her apparition was seen.

In cases of this type, it cannot be told with certainty whether the person whose apparition was seen actually died before or after the incident occurred. If the apparitions seen were sighted before death then, obviously, astral projection is implied.

In *The Unknown* by Professor Flammarion (Harper & Bros., 1900), Case XIII provides a luminous apparition. The percipient wrote that while lying in bed at night he saw a "shadowy, luminous" form which floated to him and smiled. He called aloud the name of Leontine, which was the name of a little girl who was sick and could not recover. He called a few days later at the village where she lived and discovered that she had died the day and hour that he had seen her apparition.

It will be noticed that the "shadowy, luminous" form which had been seen is remarkably like Margrave's projected astral double described in Lord Bulwer-Lytton's *A Strange Story*. I think it is clear that the author had either talked to someone who had experienced just such an apparition or had read appropriate literature on the subject.

From *Death and Its Mystery: At the Moment of Death* by Flammarion (T. Fisher Unwin, 1922), an example of a luminous disk of light heralding a death is given (p. 134). A woman was awakened by the violent opening of a dining-room window. She closed it and returned to bed, where she then saw a luminous, distorted disk of soft light on a wall. Later in the morning a dining-room table spontaneously split along its length. The narrator's father was ill at the time and died about forty-eight hours after the table split.

This case is a bit more complex than most in that it apparently included physical phenomena. The relationship of such effects to poltergeist phenomena is interesting.

Flammarion included an example of a luminous disk with an accompanying figure in *The Unknown*. In Case CXXXII, B., the writer (a woman), woke during the night and saw a circular area of light surrounding an upright figure. She recognized the form as her husband's brother, who spoke to her saying that he had died. The following day a telegram was received telling of his death. The time, unfortunately, was not specified.

A rather unusual example is given in Flammarion's *Death and Its Mystery: At the Moment of Death* (pp. 111–15), which describes how a woman entered a carriage and saw within it a light which she said was faint and gray. It grew brighter and within its confines was seen a dimly defined silhouette of a semi-transparent face. She did not recognize the face, which did seem familiar, but later found out that the original of the apparition (a man), now remembered, died two days after the phantom was seen. Flammarion points out that at the time of the appearance of the phantom the man was very ill and was actually in a state of coma.

In this case, the suggestion that the dying man extruded an astral double which was seen in the carriage seems the sim-

plest and most adequate solution. Of course, involved telepathic theories can be forced to fit the mold but they are
easily seen to be far less probable and become very cumber-
some.

An interesting case which featured both a luminosity and a
clearly seen face is found in Mrs. Sidgwick's *Phantasms of the
Living* (L 1076). In this example the subject saw a blue and
luminous mist which gradually approached her bed. When it
had reached the bedside, the percipient, who was reading a
book, suddenly saw over the top of her book the brow and
eyes of a friend. This friend had attempted to project himself
to the viewer, and the time of his attempt and the viewing of
the luminous mist and the apparition coincided.

In another case from the same work (L 1187), the viewer
saw a friend, Miss Steele, appear in an area of bright light.
The apparition in this case was not self-luminous but appeared as she would if she had been seen normally in day-
light. Miss Steele at the time of the incident was alive. Again,
projection is implied, even though telepathic explanations
can be given to explain the incident.

Certain observations made by Sir William Crookes in *Researches into Spiritualism* regarding materialization effects are
very appropriate and shed more light upon certain aspects of
luminous phenomena. He noted the interesting fact that
some witnesses saw one thing and others an entirely different
manifestation. This fact has, of course, direct bearing upon
the "subjective" nature of many psychical manifestations.

Crookes notes: "The hands and fingers do not always appear to me to be solid and life-like. Sometimes, indeed, they
present more the appearance of a nebulous cloud partly con-
densed into the form of a hand. This is not equally visible to

all present. For instance, a flower or other small object is seen to move; one person present will see a luminous cloud hovering over it, another will detect a nebulous-looking hand, while others will see nothing at all but the moving flower. I have more than once seen, first an object move, then a luminous cloud appear to form about it, and, lastly, the cloud condense into shape and become a perfectly-formed hand . . . at the wrist, or arm, it becomes hazy and fades off into a luminous cloud."

Stainton Moses also gave interesting observations regarding this same point (*Proceedings*: S.P.R., Vol. IX, pp. 311–12). During a sitting with Dr. and Mrs. Speer, Moses saw clouds of light which gathered into a columnar shape and then took the form of a stately figure. The figure pointed toward Moses, then stepped toward him, and finally dissolved into a luminous mist. Dr. Speer and his wife, on the other hand, saw only a misty luminescence.

The fact that the Speers saw something, even though quite different from Moses's "vision," indicates that the phenomenon observed was still objective to some degree in that all witnesses saw it. Naturally, there is no possible way to tell if what Moses saw was partially the product of his own mind—a subjective vision of the figure.

Appropriate to the ability, to call it that, of a luminous psychical manifestation to appear modified to different observers, some few years ago Mr. Attila von Szalay and I were sitting in a dark room performing certain experiments, when I saw what can be described as waves of violet passing down before my eyes. As I watched, these waves gradually encompassed me so that I seemed to be completely surrounded by a beautiful sea of violet light. I quickly noticed that I saw the incredible luminous field with my eyes shut as well as open and I assumed that I was experiencing some form of subjective effect produced by our experiment. However, when our sitting was finished Mr. von Szalay stated that he had seen white light.

I think it safe to say that during this incident we both saw collectively a luminous effect. It can be said to have been partially subjective in that each saw a different manifestation, but objective in that it was seen collectively. Of course, it can be regarded as the result of telepathic transmission. (If one prefers, the "mechanism" of a telepathic "field" can replace the word "transmission." Some contemporary researchers prefer this newer interpretation.)

One last illustration, very well known, will be given which provides a luminous phenomenon of a somewhat different nature and of openly spiritistic nature. The case (332) is given in *Phantasms of the Living*, and was furnished by the Reverend C. Jupp. Briefly, a man died leaving his family in desperate circumstances. A few years later his wife also died, and her younger children were placed in an orphanage. One night the superintendent who, of necessity, slept in the younger children's dormitory, woke suddenly for no apparent reason, and saw a small cloud of light floating over the youngest child. In the morning, as the superintendent started to dress the children, the little boy said that his mother had come to him and asked the superintendent if he too had seen her.

Clearly, luminous phenomena come in many forms and are frequently associated with either death or "astral projection." Light effects also seem to be associated with mediumistic phenomena in general and are encountered both spontaneously and in the séance room.

CHAPTER SIX

PHANTASMIC

REFLECTIONS

AN ODD but thoroughly interesting facet of apparitional manifestations are the reflections of faces and figures which have been seen in mirrors and on the surfaces of objects such as tables and cabinets. Phantasmic faces have been seen on rougher surfaces, but this fact immediately indicates that they were not reflections. This phenomenon, to lump several effects under one heading, at times has definite bearing on the question of the objectivity of apparitions.

The well-known case of the apparition and its reflection seen in a mirror by Lady B. and her daughter recounted in Chapter Two is a case in point. The phantom was seen both in the room and reflected in a mirror. As we have seen, both phantom and reflection were seen according to the correct perspective and parallax.

The above case was given in *The Enigma of Survival* by Professor Hornell Hart to illustrate, with other cases, his contention that phantasms are semiobjective "objects" which exist independently of their viewers, contrary to the hypothesis that they are nonobjective and the result of a telepathic process.

Almost exactly to the contrary, Case MCL 103 in the February, 1905, *Journal*: S.P.R. provided several phantasmic figures followed by a scene of a long hallway which opened into a brilliantly illuminated room in which more figures were seen. Several witnesses collectively saw these various visions, which were initiated by a mist which apparently rose before a medium who was present, and transmuted itself into a likeness of a known person. These different visions were all seen reflected in a small mirror on a bedroom wall.

Obviously, the visions seen in this case were not objective, and the *Journal* states that the incident resembles collectively viewed visions seen in crystals. It is also stated that the four witnesses had impressions closely approximating each other and represented an example of "collective hallucination." The question of nonphysical, psychical sight must also be considered.

These two cases representing phenomena differing widely yet featuring apparitional forms seen in mirrors show clearly the great range covered by such incidents.

In the *Journal*: S.P.R., 1906, a very interesting, collectively viewed apparition is reported by the Reverend Charles L. Tweedale. One night he woke and found himself looking at the panels of a wardrobe built into the wall of his bedroom. The wooden panels were illuminated by moonlight and, as he looked, he saw an apparitional face form on them. It was dimly seen at first but gradually became more distinct until he saw the face of his grandmother clearly. The phantasm was seen at about 2:00 a.m.

His father and his aunt also saw an apparition of the grandmother—his father saw it in the night, and his aunt saw it about eighteen hours after the grandmother's death, which had occurred at 12:15 a.m. the same night that her apparition appeared to Tweedale.

A contribution by Prince Duleep Singh, given in the *Journal: S.P.R.*, December, 1894 (L 977), describes how he found himself, after going to bed, looking at a print, an oleograph, on the wall. As he watched, he suddenly saw the face of his father within the confines of the frame. Prince Singh said that the apparitional face did not look like a picture but was completely lifelike and looked back at him with an intense expression.

The following morning he told Lord Carnarvon about the incident, and that evening Lord Carnarvon brought him the news of his father's death, which had taken place during the evening of the previous day.

One last case of this general type is taken from Eleanor Sidgwick's *Phantasms of the Living* (331). Seven witnesses in all saw the appearance of a man, about six weeks after his death, on the shiny surface of a wardrobe. It was described as appearing similar to a "medallion portrait" showing head, part of the arms, and shoulders.

It is nearly a literary tradition to have ghostly faces peering through windows at astonished onlookers, and, as with much of psychical tradition, the legend reflects reality.

An interesting case is given of an apparition seen in a window by a witness, who then described her experience to two others. It was later discovered that the apparition was that of a friend who had been slightly injured in an accident. He was lying on a couch the day following his accident wondering if the percipient was aware of the incident. In the midst of these thoughts he heard her voice, apparently originating from the outside of his house, and was very much surprised to find that she was not there.

The simplest explanation that can be offered in a case of

this type is that of astral projection—that is, the injured man projected his double to the window where "he" was seen. Alternative explanations involve telepathic mechanisms.

Another case of a similar nature is given in the *Journal*: S.P.R., December, 1893 (L 962). The witness described how he was engaged in writing when he happened to turn his head to a nearby window, where he saw the face of a young girl who lived twenty or twenty-five miles away. Inquiry revealed that the girl and her mother had, at the time of the vision, been engaged in a conversation about him, which the writer assures us was quite unusual.

In cases of this type and in those featuring phantom figures seen through windows, it does seem that they are not in the nature of a "reflection" or appearances forming on the surface of objects by an unknown mechanism, but are what they seem to be: figures possessing some degree of objectivity which are placed on the other side of windows through which they are seen. Assuming for the moment that the two cases presenting visions of living persons do represent viewings of extruded "astral doubles," then semiobjective beings have been seen with normal vision.

If a telepathic hypothesis is preferred, then the figures seen represent nonobjective products of a hallucinatory process triggered by a paranormal mechanism. However, I believe that evidence is now available which tips the scales decisively, in many cases, to the real object side.

CHAPTER SEVEN

PHYSICAL

PHENOMENA

NEARLY all phases of psychical phenomena provide some form of physical manifestation. Such effects are part and parcel of the séance and occur in many forms in spontaneous happenings. Naturally, cases of poltergeist are examples of objective manifestations par excellence, and a great percentage of hauntings are replete with real sounds, moving objects, touches, etc. The subject proper of apparitions is inextricably interwoven with objective phenomena which cannot be separated from phantasmic manifestations.

Many effects accompany visible apparitions—I say visible because, even though an actual figure may not be seen, still the manifestations which frequently occur so clearly represent an unseen, though objective, being, that it is hard to resist the belief that an invisible figure is also present—ranging from the sound of footsteps to the disturbance of physical objects. As with much psychical phenomena, these manifestations often occur about the time of death.

I will begin a description of the various phenomena associated with apparitional activity with a reasonably recent case which I personally studied. I have offered this incident in previous works, but will cite it again because it illustrates a particularly interesting point.

At 5:45 p.m. on June 7, 1944, I was seated with a friend in her house in Eagle Rock having coffee in the breakfast room. I heard the lock of the front door operate and the door swing open. Without thinking, I rose to answer the door, when my friend remarked, "That's only the ghost." The oddity of this sentence did not strike me at first. I assumed that she was jesting, and I walked through the dining room to the small entrance hall, which was well illuminated. As soon as I had passed into this hallway area, I clearly heard the front door close. I approached within a few feet of the door and, to my utter astonishment, heard three footsteps progress from the door into the carpeted hallway. The footsteps were perfectly audible and were within a very few feet of where I was standing. But, in spite of the good lighting and the obvious fact that something apparently had walked past me, nothing was to be seen.

At first glance, one would think that an invisible being had walked in and past me, but the fact that the front door had never actually been opened shows that the sounds cannot be "taken" literally. In all possibility, the footsteps, even though capable of being heard by my friend, were not in an ordinary sense truly objective. But they were not subjective either in the sense of representing some type of psychically originated hallucinatory experience which was collectively heard. This problem will be discussed later.

Noises found in many cases of spontaneous phenomena providing apparitional activity are paralleled in examples of haunting and poltergeist which, on the face of it, present concrete, physical actions, but upon investigation do not reflect actual happenings. The famed Willington Mill Haunting (or poltergeist haunting, if one prefers) featured visible apparitions and furnished sounds of all description, paranormal movement of objects, vocal effects, etc., and many of the sounds which were heard did not prove to have been accompanied by physical happenings.

For example, during the earlier stages of the haunting, the loud sound of the wheels of a wooden cistern, which rode on iron wheels, was heard by the foreman of the mill during the night. He immediately searched and found that the device had never stirred from its proper place.

According to the diary of Mr. Edmund Proctor, who was the owner and occupant of the mill-house, the sound of footsteps was heard more than once on a gravel walk when nothing could be seen. There were one or two other witnesses to these incidents which, in the language of *Phantasms of the Living*, apparently were collective auditory hallucinations—a title which does not solve the problem in the least.

A bell was heard but it was proven by the occupants that no bell with this particular tone existed within the house.

During one night violent sounds were heard in the lower part of the house which seemed to have been produced by a furious intruder who was slamming doors and throwing various objects about. As usual, when an investigation was made, nothing was found out of place.

These few examples taken from the multitude of manifestations which occurred in the haunted mill are typical of the entire case and provide fine samplings of sounds unmatched by a corresponding physical reality. The story of the haunting is given in the *Journal*: S.P.R., Vol. V, 1891–92, and in Chapter XV of *Poltergeist over England* (Country Life Ltd., 1945) by Harry Price.

Another example of mysterious sounds unmatched by actual events is taken from Flammarion's *Haunted Houses* (D. Appleton & Co., 1924) which describes how extraordinary noises were heard in the kitchen of a girls' school. There were sounds of the smashing of crockery, etc. A later search revealed that nothing had been disturbed in the kitchen. Incidentally, the building was blessed by a priest in order to put an end to the manifestations, but to no avail.

The sound of speech is frequently heard in the presence of apparitions which cannot be related to physical fact. To dip again into that marvelous well of apparitional evidence, *Phantasms of the Living*, Mrs. Clerke (Case 242) reported that, when she was seated on the veranda of her home in Barbados, her Negro nurse asked her who the man was who had just been speaking to her. Mrs. Clerke said that she had neither seen nor heard anyone, but, at the suggestion of the nurse, wrote down the day. Later she received news that her brother had died at about the time the apparition had been seen and heard by the nurse.

It is plain that both visual effect and sound in this case did not reflect normal physical reality, inasmuch as both effects were noted only by the nurse.

In *Death and Its Mystery: At the Moment of Death*, a case is presented which tells how a percipient had dozed off and was awakened by feeling as if his chest had been pressed. He lifted himself upon one elbow and, opening his eyes, saw his grandmother, who said that she had come to say farewell and that he would not see her again.

It was discovered that the writer's grandmother, while dying, had repeatedly said that her grandson would never see her again.

This incident reminds me of visual phenomena which

occur in the presence of Mr. Attila von Szalay, a possessor of considerable mediumistic abilities. To digress for a moment —he frequently reports that he sees violet lights in the presence of various people, including me. In these cases, I have never seen one, but a most skeptical man who is interested in psychism admitted to me that, as Mr. von Szalay started to remark that he had just seen such a light, he also saw it at the other end of the room. He described it as a large, shimmering patch of violet light. I was present during this incident, but saw nothing.

In another incident, a young lady whom I knew indicated to me that she had seen violet lights just before Mr. von Szalay reported them.

It can be seen, therefore, that the lights undoubtedly have, in a sense, some objectivity, unless one wishes to interpret such incidents as the result of telepathically instigated hallucinations. I will state at this point that I do not believe this theory will apply to happenings of this type, and that in my opinion the "percipients" are constituted so that they are capable of sensing phenomena belonging to a "psychical world."

The fact that numerous apparitions are seen by one person and not another, the fact that sounds are heard which clearly are not the product of actual physical happenings, the fact that not only apparitions appear of human beings and animals but also of vehicles, rooms, houses, and scenery led G. N. M. Tyrrell to formulate his somewhat baffling theory of hallucinations triggered by paranormal processes, which he entitled the "stage carpenter." This incredible and all-inclusive theory is equaled in scope only by the "super-ESP theory" and can in turn only be matched by Deity. Its main foundation crumbles when faced with the fact that, on occasion, apparitions have influenced physical matter, demonstrating beyond doubt that some phantasms are constructed of semiphysical material capable of reflecting light, casting shadows, etc. Tyrrell's suggestions are given in *Apparitions*, originally published in 1953 by the [English] Society for Psychical Research and reprinted by University Books Inc. in 1961.

A very common form of psychical phenomena is the hearing of noises during the period surrounding death. In spite of the fact that, in a vast percentage of such cases, visible apparitions are not seen, many incidents suggest the presence of unseen "beings." Other cases have provided sounds which seem to have been thoroughly objective and were collectively heard. Examples of such sound phenomena are present in the following incidents.

In Letter 815 from *Death and Its Mystery: At the Moment of Death*, a priest wrote that, on the night of the death of the great-grandmother of a pupil, he woke from sleep to hear a "terrible cry" which he recognized as the voice of his friend. The following morning he was told that she had died at about the same time he had heard the fearful sound and at the moment of her death had given a "great cry." Naturally, the priestly percipient could not have heard the actual cry: She lived twenty minutes away in terms of walking distance, and so the sound must be classified as subjective in nature.

These few cases are sufficient to indicate the fact that many sounds representing death and in some cases apparitional activity are not truly objective and frequently indicate apparitional activity in the sense that an "invisible" apparition is suggested.

A case in point is given in *Death and Its Mystery: At the Moment of Death* (p. 143). The writer told how she and a friend had visited an old friend who was very ill and on the verge of death. They returned home, and during the following morning heard and saw the bedroom door shaken strongly. A second period of shaking occurred, and both women returned to the bedside of their friend. They assumed that the actions of the door had heralded death, but they found their friend still alive. However, she did die two or three hours after the event. Since both women were present and signed the report describing the incident, it represents a typical collective experience of this genre.

A very interesting, collectively experienced incident is also given in the same work (p. 310). The writer told how his mother was awakened from her sleep in October, 1918, and felt the pressure of a hand gripping her wrist. At the same time a cracking sound of loud volume seemingly originated from the bedroom door. She awakened her husband and told him· what had happened, and expressed fears about her mother, who had not been well.

In this case, the impression is gained that a definite objective phenomenon was encountered when the cracking noise was heard emanating from the door. The feeling of pressure by an unseen hand, a most common effect which includes touches of all description, can be considered a tactile hallucination engendered by a telepathic process. There seems to be no good reason why such cannot occur. But to interpret all cases where touches are felt as tactile hallucinations is, I think, unwise, particularly in the light of the evidence for astral projection, and the immensely significant researches of Dr. Robert Crookall in this field.

An interesting case which included phenomena similar to those encountered with the poltergeist is given (on pp. 290–92) in *Haunted Houses* by Flammarion. A few days after the death of the writer's wife's maternal grandfather, various odd sounds were heard which gave every indication of having been objective in nature. The sounds of pebbles thrown at the windows were heard, the sound of a shovel working at a coal pile occurred, the latch of the door mechanism "seemed" to operate, and in desperation a woman spoke loudly asking the dead man to speak to the witnesses.

Interestingly, the phenomena apparently were triggered when a "forbidden to be touched" trunk was opened and a plait of hair belonging to the dead man's wife was burned.

This last item, the destruction of the plait of hair and the opening of the trunk, does perhaps seem to be a traditional touch, but it could very well have been completely factual, particularly when the poltergeistlike nature of the reported incident is remembered.

Perhaps at this point it might be well to comment on the characteristic of cases which have been drawn from the works of Professor Camille Flammarion. It will be noticed, I am sure, that in the cases included in his collection of paranormal incidents, often the phenomena reported are somewhat more "intense" than those described in, say, *Phantasms of the Living*. With spontaneous manifestations coinciding with death, with illness, etc., more objective effects are detailed, including raps, lights, touches, sounds, and so on. It might be said that the accounts compiled by Flammarion presenting more "exotic" phenomena are simply due to lower standards in accepting cases. It might also be suggested that national differences, a more volatile nature, might well account for the variance.

This last suggestion might actually play a part in the difference noted, but not necessarily in the sense that the people of one nation are more prone to exaggeration than those of another nation. It could well be that a more emotionally open nature might result in a heightened susceptibility to forces producing psychical phenomena of a physical order. This possibility cannot be ignored.

As for the possibility of lower standards having been adopted, it can be safely said that Flammarion's cases were not as rigidly screened as were the cases accepted by the authors of *Phantasms of the Living*. This does not in the least imply that his cases are unworthy of consideration—far from that—but it does imply that in some examples exaggerations and imaginative material might have crept in, and undoubtedly some cases must be fraudulent. However, in any collection, no matter how well screened, fraud, to some extent, will find an entry and some imaginative material will be present. But this is true of any scientific field, and an examination of general experimental work will reveal a number of hoaxes, slipshod work, and open mistakes.

For example, I am familiar with the case of a noted parapsychologist on the West Coast who was scoring an ESP test. A fellow researcher who was aiding in the scoring found that the parapsychologist had made a number of mistakes. These tests would have been accepted in the general literature of the field except for this discovery, and the possibility exists that other errors were passed by. The same parapsychologist had been engaged in "mediumistic" sittings, had become "entranced" and portrayed a "spirit," and tipped tables in a thoroughly "naïve" manner. This is distressing but, as I noted earlier, the other sciences are also no stranger to questionable practices and extraordinary errors.

However, Professor Flammarion's cases are sufficiently numerous and in many examples sufficiently screened to render them acceptable for use. In his *Haunted Houses* (English version, 1924) he mentioned that he had collected cases including noises, the sound of keys operating in locks, and the sound of footsteps, cries, etc., to the vast number of more than 5,600. As Flammarion remarks, it would be foolish to attempt to say that all were the product of practical jokers.

Professor Flammarion wrote that in his books he was only able to present summaries and extracts, and was unable to publish complete observations and verifications. The reason for this was the simple lack of space—a perfectly valid reason. If the reader of such cases wishes to study the complete material, then the original reports should be consulted. Flammarion did note that in some cases, due to sentimental and family reasons, confirmatory material was not sent to him—a common and unfortunate obstacle found in the study of certain effects. This same obstacle was encountered with the Piper case, and much material of great importance will never be available for study.

For example, Hodgson wrote in "A Further Record of Observations of Certain Phenomena of Trance," *Proceedings*: A.S.P.R., XXXIII, Vol. XIII, 1893: "Of the written reports of first sittings there are many which I am practically unable to use as evidence, owing to the reluctance of the sitters to allow the private matters concerned to be published in any form. There are others which I could publish only under such restrictions and with such alterations that they would lose much of their significance."

In essence, Professor Flammarion's cases follow the typical pattern of spontaneous psychical occurrences which display more objective features and cannot be said to diverge from this standard in any way. Professor Hornell Hart thought enough of them to remark in his work that from 1900 to 1923 Flammarion continued to collect cases of this type. This reference was made in Hart's "Psychical Research and the Methods of Science," *Journal*: A.S.P.R., July, 1957, and so I see little reason to omit the use of his cases.

From *Death and Its Mystery: After Death* (Letter 2358) I take a case in which the writer told how his father, after his death, and according to a previous agreement, presumably broke a window glass by means of a horizontal, unbending crack. When the window cracked, it emitted a loud noise like a gunshot. A clock struck the hours in a fashion which was entirely slower than normal and continued this action for a few weeks.

As written, the sounds heard in this case were clearly objective in nature. So were certain other events which occurred.

From the same work (Letter 1066) the writer tells that about eight days after his wife's maternal grandfather, who lived in his home, died, a bell in the house began to ring. The room in which the bell was located had been closed since the burial. The entire family and a servant dashed into the room and saw that the cord to the bell still vibrated. This effect was repeated twice more.

In a case of this type there is direct evidence that the sounds heard were objective and the vibration of the bell cord, by this action, verified the entirely physical nature of the bell ringing.

Many cases which have featured visible phantoms and many cases which offer evidence of "invisible" apparitional activity provide the sensation of pressure, of contact by unseen hands, and so on.

From *Death and Its Mystery: After Death* (The Century Co., 1923, p. 243), a woman was sewing, accompanied by her cat, who was resting on a chair close-by. The cat suddenly rose, looked to one side, and made a spitting noise. At the same time the narrator heard a voice call her name and felt a sensation as though a hand had heavily pressed her shoulder.

The narrator's great-uncle had died two months previously, but no abnormal incidents had occurred before the event described.

Unless one wishes to ascribe to the cat a telepathic reception of a transmission from her mistress, its reactions strongly imply that a certain degree of objectivity was present with the phenomena encountered.

A case which Hereward Carrington thought well enough of to include in his *Psychic World* (G. P. Putnam's Sons, 1937) was originally published in *Experiences of a New Guinea Resident Magistrate* by Captain A. W. Monckton (p. 109).

The narrator was seated and writing when he heard the sound of footsteps on a coral walkway outside the house in which he was staying. The footsteps progressed to the veranda and walked through his room, which was well lighted.

The same sounds occurred again and in the same pattern and apparently behind his chair. Captain Monckton wrote that it sounded exactly as though a living person had walked through the room, and he paid little attention to them.

Then two doors which he had previously closed were opened, and the puzzled magistrate carefully closed them once more. At the same time he realized that nothing could be seen to explain the strange footsteps.

After more puzzling effects, Captain Monckton, with his servants, heard the footsteps again walk over the coral path, across the veranda and through his room.

As the footsteps advanced across the veranda, he carefully noticed that the flexible floor of the veranda, which was floored with palm, depressed with each footstep.

A previous occupant had made allusions to odd happenings and said that he too had heard the phantasmic footsteps on occasion.

Again, I do not see how the admission that an "invisible apparition" had walked across Captain Monckton's floor can be avoided. The depression of the flooring under each footstep proved, beyond any reasonable doubt, that the "being," which must have been sufficiently humanlike in form to produce realistic-sounding footsteps, was certainly solid in that it possessed weight and could exert physical pressure.

It can be seen that physical phenomena do occur in the presence of apparitions and apparitional activity, as well as in the experimental séance room, and can occur in many modes. In this chapter a number of the most common varieties have been outlined and will, I hope, provide a sufficiently encompassing picture of such manifestations.

CHAPTER EIGHT

POLTERGEISTS,

HAUNTINGS,

AND APPARITIONS

THE PRESENCE of apparitions in haunting cases is traditional, and almost all proper and satisfying ghost stories have a visible phantom to round them out. Perhaps not quite so well known are the reports of phantoms with poltergeist disturbances, but this fact might well be due to the disputed classification of these closely related manifestations.

To define the poltergeist, I will present a few designations which may or may not clarify the situation. For instance, A. R. G. Owen in *Can We Explain the Poltergeist?* (a book including some valuable information but one which is limited and reflects little personal experience with such phenomena) defines such activity as the production of spontaneously occurring sounds such as thumpings and knockings, and the movement of objects in a manner unexplainable for normal causes. He did discuss other effects and the possibility that they do actually exist.

This definition is clearly inadequate. Following Owen's thought, practically any séance phenomena, providing physical phenomena, could be labeled poltergeist activity.

By the same token, any case of indisputable haunting could also be labeled a poltergeist infestation.

Hereward Carrington, in *Haunted People, the Story of the Poltergeist Down the Ages* (co-authored by Nandor Fodor), first defined the poltergeist case as disturbances in which kitchenware is smashed, bells are mysteriously rung, and various objects of all description are tossed about apparently by an unseen force. Carrington continues and lists the many phenomena found with cases of this kind. He refers to spontaneous fires, stone throwings so typical of the poltergeist, the slow actions of objects traveling through the air, the fact that such objects do not necessarily follow a straight path, the fact that on occasions thrown objects are abnormally warm, the passage of objects through solid matter such as walls and closed doors (called apports), the sprinkling of water, voices, visible apparitions—in short, the entire gamut of poltergeist phenomena. Carrington also noted the connection of the poltergeist with a psychical energy emerging from the physical body which is connected with the maturing of the sexual functions. He advanced this theory in *The Story of Psychic Science* (1931).

In my opinion, Hereward Carrington was not favorable to the spiritistic theory of survival and consequently could not have believed that poltergeist activities were produced by independent entities. I drove him home one evening from a friend's home and I asked him point-blank if he thought that survival of death was fact. He replied that he did not. It must be noted, however, that in his books he always admitted the possibility of survival and the rationality of this theory. At one time he openly championed the spiritistic theory and in his work, *Eusapia Palladino and Her Phenomena*, stated that her psychical effects could only be properly explained by surviving spirits.

In *Ghosts and Poltergeists*, Father Herbert Thurston quickly defines the poltergeist as a "spirit" which tosses things about, and, in general, creates a glorious disturbance. He notes that on rare occasions people are struck by thrown objects but practically never are seriously injured. He also includes throughout his book a list, so to speak, of the other effects which are found with the poltergeist, which include all the manifestations mentioned by Carrington.

As to final conclusions, Father Thurston writes that he is convinced that such phenomena do occur and states that they prove the existence of a nonphysical world, a sphere of what he terms "spiritual agencies." However, he insists that he is not called upon to provide final theories and remarks that he does not think that one need invoke diabolic forces in explanation.

In *Poltergeist over England*, Harry Price defines the poltergeist as a presumed spirit, an entity, a secondary personality, which possesses numerous undesirable qualities. He mentions its cruel, destructive, purposeless, noisy behavior. Price includes the entire gamut of phenomena, a thoroughly long list, which includes apparitions, footsteps, crashes, raps, movement of objects, apports, smashing of dishes and other objects, stone throwing, falling water, fires, and voices. This list, of course, concurs perfectly with that given by Mr. Carrington and Father Thurston.

Some years ago I wrote a book devoted to poltergeist and haunting phenomena (*The Enigma of the Poltergeist*) and in it I gave a list of effects found with both manifestations—a list which differs in no way from the authorities mentioned. I referred to theories which suggest that poltergeist activity is clearly influenced by psychological tensions and may well represent a curative process in that such tensions are relieved by the manifestations, and I concluded that, as with hauntings, the poltergeist may, in some cases, include in its mechanisms spiritistic influences. This last view is, of course, anathema to much of contemporary parapsychological holy writ. I also particularly made the point that it is difficult, if not impossible, to draw a sharp line between hauntings and the poltergeist and suggested that each imperceptibly blends into the other.

A very popular interpretation today is that the poltergeist represents the actions of a secondary personality utilizing paranormal abilities of the poltergeist subject or medium. The view that the phenomena found in such cases act as a curative psychological process relieving a psychological problem and as a purposeful process was advanced by Dr. John Layard in his paper, "Psi Phenomena and Poltergeists," *Proceedings*: S.P.R., July, 1944.

Nandor Fodor promulgated a psychoanalytic view which became quite well known. He postulated an actual split-off fragment of the personality acting independently which produced the various phenomena found with the poltergeist. This suggestion represents an extreme view which does not, in my opinion, reflect parapsychological reality and really suggests a form of survival.

The present parapsychological term, a kind of scientific jargonese for such phenomena, is RSPK, which means recurring spontaneous psychokinesis. In one sense the term is a good one. It is self-explanatory, but it does suffer a disadvantage in that it is most unwieldy. Further, the very term psychokinesis is not a truly correct term, since it implies that all telekinetic effects are created by the mind, a large and loose assumption. Why not use a term implying a biological origin, or perhaps one oriented toward physics? To attempt to corral all psychical phenomena in the psychological mold may represent good strategy on the part of those involved in this field, but it most certainly does not reflect scientific accuracy.

Among truly knowledgeable researchers today, I doubt if one will find many who seriously resist the thought that poltergeist (and haunting) phenomena are a reality. A vast amount of material now is available which testifies to the actuality of such phenomena, and recent cases have been studied firsthand by a number of eminent parapsychologists.

As I remarked in another chapter, I, too, have personally observed two such cases "in action," have witnessed spontaneous phenomena on several occasions, and have studied several cases "on location" even though they were not active at the moment. In view of the tremendous store of good evidence attesting to the reality of such cases, I do not believe that any person, seriously and open-mindedly studying this material, can emerge from his studies without admitting that cases of this type do occur which have been examined carefully and adequately.

Apropos of the older attitude regarding the existence of poltergeist phenomena, D. J. West wrote in his paper, "The Investigation of Spontaneous Cases," *Proceedings*: S.P.R., Vol. XLVIII, Part 175, July, 1948, that a conformity to a tradition such as witchcraft and magic does not in the least mean that good evidence for their reality has been provided. Far from that. Conformity to legend, then, is certainly no guarantee of fact.

West wrote that tales of magic and witchcraft follow a

common pattern, but in spite of this semblance of conformity, we do not automatically accept them as fact.

He stated that the "ill-reputed" poltergeist case follows a universal pattern probably more closely than does any type of ghostly manifestation. In fact, he notes that "thorybism," or apparently abnormal stone-throwing and other phenomena, is reported continually and from all over the world, and that the resemblance between cases of the past and present is truly uncanny. He wrote that the poltergeist is the one kind of haunting most denigrated and distrusted by parapsychological investigators.

All of this clearly shows that the mere fact that a body of researchers does not like a particular type of phenomena does not in the least mean that it is nonexistent. For example, West further commented that the odd legend of the poltergeist has endured over centuries but that fact is no more remarkable than is the continuance of folklore.

At the time he wrote this paper, the intellectual climate was such that acceptance of the poltergeist could not exist with a large number of researchers. In fact, the entire subject of physical phenomena has never really been viewed with favor by the Society for Psychical Research in England. A very pronounced example of this can be found with the resistance by Miss Johnson to the findings of Hereward Carrington, Everard Fielding, and W. W. Baggally with Eusapia Palladino. She, rather than admit that physical phenomena did occur with this noted medium, preferred (along with Mrs. Sidgwick) to suggest that the experimenters were hallucinated. This ridiculous idea eventually fell by the wayside. Since I have had the pleasure of knowing Hereward Carrington, the very thought of his having been strangely subject to hallucination only when he saw physical phenomena and was in the séance room with Palladino, is so completely foolish that it can only provoke laughter.

Hauntings, to utilize a most arbitrary definition for the moment, are considered by some to be not destructive in their behavior and are traditionally confined to a house, an office, a church, a ship, etc., and are presumably confined to a place. The manifestations found with such cases are very similar to those with the poltergeist and include apparitions, the sound of voices and even instruments, footsteps, movement of objects, rappings and poundings, luminous effects, odors, sprinkling of water, and so on. Spontaneous fires and stone throwings, for instance, are not generally considered to be a part of haunting cases, but it can be easily seen that categories merge into one general type. As I mentioned, I find it hard, if not impossible, to separate one from the other. Perhaps one difference is that the poltergeist usually centers on a child or an adolescent, although there are even exceptions to that.

The Willington Mill poltergeist/haunting or, if one please, haunting proper (Harry Price lists it as a case of poltergeist) began in 1835 and continued for many years. The best-known source of material is the diary of Mr. Joseph Proctor, and the report of his son, Mr. Edmund Proctor, which were published in the *Journal*: S.P.R., Vol. V, 1891–92. Other reports of this remarkable disturbance are given in William Stead's *More Ghost Stories*, and Catherine Crowe's *Night Side of Nature*.

The case began when mysterious sounds were heard in the house. A nursemaid, a kitchen worker, and others insisted that they had heard heavy footsteps in a room which was not used, and soon all members of the family had heard them also. The sounds gradually increased in intensity and variety, and eventually knockings and other sounds were heard, including those of whistles, furniture being moved about, a nonexistent bell ringing, voices, rustlings, etc.

Apparitions were seen both singly and collectively. A luminous figure was seen at a window by the foreman of the mill and his wife. This appearance was also witnessed by two other observers. A phantasmic figure (previously mentioned) was seen which snuffed out a candle. A Dr. Drury, who wished to experience the haunting, saw "the G" (ghost) and actually fainted from shock. The children saw phantasmic appearances, including the form of a monkeylike apparition. In his diary, Mr. Proctor comments that, even though he was a very young child at the time, he definitely remembered seeing this strange apparition.

After the Proctors left the haunted house, it was divided into two dwellings, and the foreman lived in one. He reported seeing apparitional forms, and other families who moved in about 1867 were seriously disturbed. Eventually, the phenomena ceased.

With activity of this type, particularly when it is remembered that apparitions were seen, including a report of the apparitional figure who snuffed out a lighted candle—a most objective action—it becomes highly possible and even probable that a certain percentage of the phenomena encountered were instigated by semiobjective, "invisible" apparitional structures. In other words, in cases of haunting and poltergeist, where stones are thrown and dishes smashed, and so on, it is logical to assume that invisible, semiphysical structures such as ectoplasmic hands or even entire figures have performed these acts.

When stones are thrown or household articles are moved or tossed about, it is evading the issue to say that a "force" or, equally vague and meaningless, "power" has been the cause. I cannot see how a "force" or a "field" can manage delicately to pick up an object and move it through space with precision without fingers or equivalent structures.

On the other hand, reasonable theories can be extracted from cases of experimental ectoplasmic phenomena observed with Eusapia Palladino or Kathleen Goligher, or touches and even complete table levitations experienced in personal experiments. Ectoplasmic forms have been witnessed and studied by highly experienced researchers such as Professor Charles Richet, Sir Oliver Lodge, Hereward Carrington, Everard Fielding, W. W. Baggally, Professor Camille Flammarion, Dr. Joseph Venzano, Professor Enrico Morselli, Dr. W. J. Crawford, Professor Cesare Lombroso, Baron von Schrenck-Notzing, Harry Price, and a host of other skilled scientists. I must add that I have also had the extremely good fortune to witness an ectoplasmic "arm" spontaneously extruded from a dark recess in the presence of Mr. Attila von Szalay, a friend and nonprofessional medium. He was standing about fifteen feet from the "arm" at the time it appeared. In view of the obvious similarity to experimental ectoplasmic forms, which not only include hands with no apparent arms or bodies attached, but entire phantasmic figures, I suggest that highly alike structures are present during many manifestations found in hauntings and cases of poltergeists. The presence of "invisible" hands and so on will solve the mystery of the puzzling movement of objects seen with such cases and provides a reasonable, working theory. Further, this concept agrees fully with the schematic (the use of the "vehicle of vitality," the semi-solid, ectoplasmic body encountered in one order of astral projection and following death) detailed by Dr. Robert Crookall.

The experiments with the medium Franek Kluski, attended by Dr. Gustave Geley, Professor Richet, Professor Flammarion, and others, resulting in the formation of the famed wax casts of materialized hands, bear directly upon this entire subject. As is a matter of psychical history, these remarkable casts were made frequently with wax that had been secretly treated with cholesterin which reacted in chemical tests, verifying that the wax gloves had not been introduced into the séances by the medium. Interestingly, on occasion, the materialized hands were occasionally luminous and consequently were very clearly experimental equivalents to luminous apparitional forms which occur at times in spontaneous cases.

The fact that the hands were capable of displacing molten wax and creating casts shows conclusively that they were, in some degree, objective in character. That the hands, at will, materialized or disappeared demonstrated that they were not composed of normal matter such as we know, and their "ectoplasmic" nature was established. They were very similar to semiobjective apparitions which have been observed in spontaneous cases and with haunting-poltergeist disturbances.

In view of these facts, I believe that the ectoplasmic mechanisms of apparitional activities are paralleled and "explained." Further, the very fact that the hands encountered with Kluski were usually invisible, but occasionally visible, exactly as are apparitional phenomena, additionally affirms the ectoplasmic theory of semiobjective hands moving objects, throwing kitchenware about, tossing stones—in short, the entire collection of effects found in poltergeist-haunting cases.

A very well-documented haunting-poltergeist disturbance occurred at a manor house built, it is believed, by Sir Thomas Stewkley before 1623 at Hinton Ampner. A descendant, Lord Stawell, owned the house and died in 1742 and, shortly following his death, a groom insisted that he had seen Lord Stawell's apparition.

The house was rented to the Ricketts family, and it is to Mrs. Mary Ricketts that we are indebted for letters describing the phenomena which beset her home. Other material also exists which describes the haunting.

After the Ricketts moved into their new home, mysterious noises and doors being slammed were soon heard. An apparitional form, a male figure, was reported twice during the first years of their occupancy.

The phantasmic figure of a woman, whose dress rustled as it swept past four witnesses who were sitting in the kitchen, was seen. A ghostly figure of a man was perceived by a groom, and the phantom, according to his description, was dressed in a "drab-colored" coat. The startled groom at first thought the figure was the new butler, but soon realized that it was an apparition.

The case, as with other disturbances of an advanced and complex order, also offered mysterious sounds of every description. Crashes, knockings, rustlings, footsteps, voices, shrieks, music—the entire gamut of ghostly sounds—were encountered in the manor house.

The Ricketts left the house, and in 1772 a family by the

name of Lawrence rented it. Apparently they also experienced some form of disturbance, since it is recorded that they made attempts to prevent their servants from talking, and it was reported that an apparition was seen. This family vacated the house in 1773, and it was destroyed after their tenancy.

Interestingly, and in the true spirit of a Gothic romance, a small unidentified skull was found under a floor when the house was being pulled down. It was, of course, rumored that a crime had taken place at the manor, but the solution of this odd puzzle is lost in the dust of years.

The famed Wesley or Epworth Rectory Haunting has been described so many times that I will only mention that apparitions which gave the appearance of small animal-like forms were reported on occasion. The usual sounds were heard, objects were physically influenced, what can be called incipient voices were heard, and the phenomena did respond to request at times.

Another noted haunting, the Ballechin House Haunting, is extremely well known, and again I will be content with the very briefest mention of the disturbance.

The house was reputed to have been haunted as far back as the year 1878 and was active in the late 1800's. It was studied by Sir Oliver Lodge, F. W. H. Myers, and others. Lodge wrote that sounds, including a wailing, knockings, a droning and sawing noises, were heard. He noted that some rappings seemed intelligent. A famed report of the case was written by Miss A. Goodrich-Freer and Lord Bute, originally titled *The Alleged Haunting of B. . . . House*, and published in London in 1899. Miss Goodrich-Freer investigated the case for about three months, and in the course of these investigations insisted that she had seen a phantom nun a number of times. Several other witnesses stated that they too had seen phantoms, though the evidence for this is perhaps a bit questionable. But the entire case was undoubtedly genuine in spite of a certain lack of evidence.

Miss Goodrich-Freer (Miss X.) also authored the well-known book, *Essays in Psychical Research*, and in this work she described her experiences with the "Hampton Court Ghost." In the interest of historical material I will brief her encounter as she described it. In Chapter 1, entitled "Haunted Houses," her "meeting" with the apparition is given in some detail. Perhaps contrary to some expectation, the haunting of this structure is probably more than mere legend, and certain reports of great interest, to the best of my knowledge, have never seen print. However, for the purpose of this book, I will remain content to mention only Miss Freer's description of her encounter with the noted phantasm.

While staying at Hampton Court Palace and after going to bed, she was awakened at four-thirty in the morning by a sound, apparently of a door opening in an empty joining room. A curious "thud" was then heard in her room, and Miss Freer, completely aroused and her investigatory instincts alert, left her bed to walk around it exploring the surrounding space.

She returned to bed preparing to attempt sleep, when she saw in the darkened room a dim, flowing light. It gradually assumed the form of a tall, slender woman, who moved across the room. The phantom passed by the foot of Miss Freer's bed and, as it did, she felt a vibration in the springs of the mattress. The phantom stopped, giving Miss Freer ample time to study it carefully.

It was dressed in an older style and, the writer observed, "Her face was insipidly pretty." Surely, these words were never said previously about an apparition and probably have never been repeated since! Even though it was possible to observe closely all the details of the phantom, Miss Freer states that she was aware that it was not substantial and was wraithlike in structure.

She asked with admirable poise if she could be of assistance, but the phantom made no reply. It stood for a short time and then raised its hands to its face, sank to its knees, and, with this action, vanished, leaving Miss Freer in a darkened room.

In this case the auditory sense was involved, in that Miss Freer first heard the odd sounds heralding the arrival of the ghost.

I have given this account primarily for its historical value. Its strict evidential value is slight inasmuch as the incident was reported by only Miss Freer herself, but it must be admitted that her account in no way violates the pattern of apparitions.

Again, it must be remembered that the ability to see apparitions and sense psychical phenomena does clearly vary with different people and, in consequence, to say that an apparition was sighted by just one person in a group of three or four does not mean that it was purely subjective in nature. One person might possess the ability to a greater degree than the others to sense paranormal effects.

A very interesting account of an apparent poltergeist-haunting which took place in southern India is included in Father Herbert Thurston's *Ghosts and Poltergeists.* (I use "A Gateway Edition," 1954, for reference.)

The case was originally described by A. S. Thangapragasm Pillay, who was a native official and a member of the Catholic Church. His account, originally written in his private diary, was not compiled for reasons of publicity, but surfaced, so to speak, when a Lieutenant Colonel O'Gorman, who had seen a description of the haunting in a local newspaper, asked Pillay to let him copy it. Colonel O'Gorman let Father Thurston use this copy, which he abridged and published in his book accompanied by other material. As described, the case represents one of the most violent poltergeist disturbances recorded and is doubly interesting inasmuch as a "diabolical" influence was also present.

The infestation began on March 3rd, and ended on March 19, 1920. It included phenomena typical in character and of a most varied order. A typical attack on all matters religious took place, and religious pictures, medals, and crucifixes were disturbed and frequently disappeared and reappeared. (This characteristic parallels the disappearance of religious articles in the Borley Rectory haunting detailed by Harry Price in *The Most Haunted House in England.*) Crosses drawn in the afflicted house for protective measures were defiled with cow dung, spontaneous fires often erupted (some of great potential danger), objects were thrown about, people received blows, stones were thrown, strange menacing messages were found scrawled on walls—a savage, "supernatural" siege was laid to Pillay's house.

On one occasion, the narrator said, he saw a figure standing in the entrance to his bedroom. Startled, he asked the mysterious visitant who she was, and the figure replied in Tamil, "Why, Father."

Granting the accuracy of the narrator's observations, the phantom's reply gave proof that it was, to some extent, aware of its interrogator, and was not a mere psychic automaton devoid of any form of consciousness.

Various religious rites were performed, and finally the infesting force left the beleaguered house. Whether the paranormal siege was lifted due to these forms of exorcism or whether it had run its course and ceased spontaneously cannot, of course, be determined.

The highly publicized haunting at Borley Rectory, studied and written about by Harry Price, has had in parapsychological literature amazing ups and downs. A number of attacks were made on the evidence Price presented for the paranormal incidents, which were claimed to have occurred at the rectory. These attacks, in a sense, culminated with the book, *The Haunting of Borley Rectory—A Critical Survey of the Evidence*, by E. J. Dingwall, K. M. Goldney, and T. H. Hall, which was published in 1956.

A few words may be appropriate at this point about the two chief critics. The third, Mrs. Goldney, seems to have regretted her part in this affair and in the *Journal: S.P.R.*, Vol. 39, had little good to say regarding the manner in which Hall and Dingwall reached conclusions.

Dingwall has become somewhat of a legend with those involved in psychical research, and his periodic, direct denials of his previous statements in print are humorous and thoroughly well known. For example, he observed genuine and splendid phenomena with Stella C. and admitted so in print. He now denies that any such phenomena exist. He wrote a special report dated June 8, 1923, in which he described the ectoplasmic structure which issued from the medium's body. In it he tells how he saw, by means of the shadow apparatus (which used a light projector and a light filter), objects placed in the path of the beam of light, and a screen upon which were thrown the shadow images of the objects between light source and screen. Dingwall lowered himself to the floor and looked under a table toward the shining screen. As he watched, he saw an egg-shaped structure, which was white, move or crawl along the floor. It was attached to the medium by a white, stringlike ectoplasmic cord. The structure moved to the center of the floor under the table and then retreated into the shadowy area. This report is reproduced in *Stella C.: An Account of Some Original Experiments in Psychical Research* (Hurst & Blackett Ltd., 1925).

Dingwall sat with "Margery" Crandon in 1925 and issued a number of opinions regarding the phenomena which he saw. His statements were contradictory.

Maurice Barbanell, Hannen Swaffer, Fred Hocking, and Dingwall in 1928 had a public debate regarding psychic phenomena; the last two participants represented the opposition. Dingwall made it known that he had never, never witnessed any psychical phenomena during his career as an investigator. Harry Price was also on the platform at this time, and, when he heard Dingwall advance this claim, he handed Swaffer a copy of a signed statement by Dingwall which attested that he had seen physical phenomena under well-controlled conditions with the medium Willie Schneider.

After this magnificent rebuttal, Price then handed Swaffer a letter, written by Dingwall, which had been sent to Baron von Schrenck-Notzing in which he described an experimental séance he had attended with "Margery." In this letter, which Swaffer read aloud, Dingwall wrote that the examples of telekinesis and ectoplasm represented the best case of its type of which he had knowledge. He further wrote that in perfectly adequate red light (he held the hands of the medium) one could hold the ectoplasmic structures in one's hands. He also admitted that the control was beyond all reproach.

Dingwall, in complaint, remarked that this admission was in a private letter. Swaffer replied that he, Dingwall, apparently held one opinion in private and another in public.

The details of this encounter are given in *Psychic News*, August 28, 1965.

As mentioned, Dingwall sat with "Margery" in 1925 and after twenty-nine sittings (it must be remembered that he had been held to be a great authority regarding the validity of psychical phenomena) he wrote in the *Proceedings*: S.P.R., Vol. XXXVI, Part 28, June, 1926, that he could come to no final conclusion about the reality or nonreality of "Margery's" phenomena. Amazing! And after twenty-nine sittings!

He has also advanced the statement that, with increased control, "mental" phenomena cease. And this he said in the face of the work with Mrs. Piper, Mrs. Leonard, Mrs. "Chenoweth," Mrs. Annie Brittain, and the numbers of other perfectly genuine mediums of this type. Such an observation cannot be taken seriously.

Trevor Hall is now identified with his unending attacks on noted psychical researchers of the past who are not around any more to reply. He has attacked Sir William Crookes, Edmund Gurney, and Miss Goodrich-Freer, to name a few, and with his sallies has at last fulfilled the famous statement that, when all else fails and psychical science cannot be sensibly discredited, then attacks will be launched on personalities. His innuendos and open attacks have been refuted in a publication of the Society for Psychical Research and by various other authorities.

The Society for Psychical Research issued a *Proceedings*: Vol. 55, Part 201, March, 1969, which is devoted to an analysis by Robert J. Hastings of the allegations launched at Harry Price by Dingwall, Hall, and Goldney. Each section of the proceedings deals with a specific implication of fraud on the part of Price.

For example, Price wrote that some bone fragments had been excavated from the cellars of Borley Rectory. His detractors implied that he had previously planted the pieces of bone before the digging took place. After an analysis of this charge, Hastings showed that this view was only the result of a number of surmises, several of which were false (p. 117).

Another section of the *Proceedings* discusses the possibility which had been raised that Price had made certain ghostly sounds by crinkling cellophane paper, but a thorough analysis ends with the statement that no evidence to this effect exists.

In his book, *The End of Borley Rectory*, Price gives a photograph of a brick apparently suspended in midair by paranormal forces. His detractors wrote that they regarded this incident in a far from favorable light. Hastings, in answer, clearly points out that Price never claimed that the brick photograph demonstrated anything of a psychical nature (p. 133).

And so it goes. Each item supposedly supporting the unreliability of Price's Borley report is disposed of, and, as a result, the haunting must again be admitted to the ranks of respectable cases worthy of study and thorough examination.

During the course of this famous haunting or poltergeist-haunting, many abnormal manifestations were reported. Voices and whisperings were heard; footsteps of every description occurred; raps and knocking of all kind took place; objects were displaced; writings were frequently found on the walls; luminous effects were witnessed; odd odors were evident; fires were set; and apparitions of several different "individuals" were seen, including the well-known "nun."

The case, in spite of the unfortunate controversy which for a time marred its reputation for validity, has again entered the ranks of the respectable, parapsychologically speaking, and is of such great interest that Price's *The Most Haunted House in England* and *The End of Borley Rectory* should be read as well as the *Proceedings*: S.P.R., March, 1969.

It is interesting to examine Price's explanations for the phenomena experienced in this well-haunted rectory. It must first be remembered that he was a loyal member of the Church of England and a religious man. This fact may come as a surprise to many, considering his noted skepticism and "toughness" as a psychical researcher. He was not, I believe it quite safe to say, an outstanding theorist, which in many cases can be an advantage. There are entirely too many parapsychologists today tossing about complex and murky theories explaining all phases of psychism, who have had little practical experience, and have not witnessed actual psychic phenomena.

A chapter in *Fifty Years of Psychical Research* (Longmans, Green and Co., 1939) titled, "I Believe . . ." gives Price's general conclusions at that time. He wrote that he did believe that buildings and places soak up certain qualities or emanations which originated from previous occupants. He also thought that some psychics, at times, can contact these emanations, which can be considered a portion of the minds of the past tenants. With this admission, he came close to spiritualistic philosophy.

Price referred to Dr. C. D. Broad's theory of what can be called "limited survival," in that a "psychic factor," a portion of a living but now deceased person, might be able to survive the blow of death for a limited time. (For the life of me, I cannot see why he tossed in a limited time. It seems a needless complexity and comes perilously close to violating the law of parsimony.) Price apparently thought somewhat the same, for he also wrote, "Why cannot this limited period be unlimited?"

Regarding the spiritualistic theory of surviving spirits and communication with the dead, he said he did not think that the spiritualists had verified their theory. But Price went on to say that the spiritistic theory did explain many of the facts observed. His reasons for not accepting the spirit hypothesis rested upon the "fact" that ostensible spirit messages have always been on the same intellectual plane as the mediums who gave them. Other reasons also entered into his consideration.

In my opinion, Price's analysis, to call it that, is very limited, and on the surface did not take into account the theories offered by Dr. Hodgson, Professor Hyslop, and others, which explain this "fact" and still uphold the survival concept. Further, I do not believe that Price's contention that mediumistic messages are on the same intellectual level as the mediums providing them will bear close scrutiny. Just the reverse has been often indicated.

However, in Chapter XXXI of *The Most Haunted House in England*, which was first published in 1940, Price wrote that persisting portions of the minds of previous occupants of Borley Rectory were responsible for the phenomena experienced. He noted that the reader could, if he wished, title such remnants, spirits. He further wrote that, all in all, the spiritistic theory explained the phenomena the best, even though certain curious manifestations cannot be adequately explained by *any* theory. Again, with such reasoning, he came extremely close to spiritualistic theory.

I do not think that Harry Price can, by any means, be considered a theorist in the terms of Dr. Robert Crookall, for example, or Professor Hornell Hart or Professor James Hyslop, but I do think that his thoughts are of interest in view of his close association with Borley Rectory.

An extraordinary poltergeist-haunting, the Phelps case, has been described in several books, including Podmore's *Modern Spiritualism*, Conan Doyle's *History of Spiritualism*, Father Thurston's *Ghosts and Poltergeists*, Fodor's *Encyclopaedia of Psychic Science*, and Carrington and Fodor's *Haunted People: The Story of the Poltergeist Down the Centuries*.

The case included phenomena which, as described, were certainly unparalleled in sheer oddity. Objects of all description were thrown about and even damaged, raps were heard, writings were found on the walls, windows were smashed, and the typically destructive actions of the poltergeist were chronicled. Even though apparitions were not actually seen during this astonishing case, strange and grotesque figures were constructed from clothing and arranged in a weird tableau. In a sense, artificial apparitions were created, and I believe that, due to the very strangeness and uniqueness of this incident, a description should be given.

The following description of the "tableau" appeared in the *New Haven Journal*, written by Dr. Webster in the form of two letters to the newspaper. The Reverend Eliakim Phelps, whose home was so oddly disturbed, endorsed the accounts.

"From this time on, the rooms were closely watched, and figures appeared when no human being could have entered the room. They were constructed and arranged, I am convinced, by no visible power, with *a tout ensemble* most beautiful and picturesque. The clothing with which the figures were constructed was somehow gathered from all parts of the house, in spite of the strict watch which was kept to see that nothing of the sort could possibly happen. In a short space of time so many figures were constructed that it would not have been possible for half a dozen women, working steadily for several hours, to have completed their design, and arrange the picturesque tableau. Yet these things happened in a short space of time, with the whole house on the watch. In all, about thirty figures were constructed during this period. Some of them were so lifelike that a small child being shown the room thought his mother was kneeling in prayer with the rest. . . ."

The accounts of the case are astonishing and near-incredible, and, at first glance, such fantastic tales seem wildly improbable. However, in the psychical realm, one soon realizes, with actual experience and not arguing from mere theory, that the weird and the apparently impossible do occur, and, with this word of caution, the next case will be considered.

Perhaps the wildest poltergeist case, according to what has been written, is the fantastic haunting of Brook House, chronicled in his diary by Mr. Ralph Hastings. The haunting, as reported, was given in Stead's *More Ghost Stories.* Edmund Gurney was interested in the case and asked Mr. Hastings to furnish him with an account of the disturbance.

The case is an extraordinary one indeed, and in sheer violence rivals and even surpasses the haunting of a Calvados castle, a noted case given in Flammarion's *Haunted Houses*, as well as in *The Annals of Psychic Science.*

On October 1, 1891, Mr. Hastings, who lived in Broadmeadow, Teignmouth, wrote to Mr. William T. Stead mentioning that he had personally witnessed the remarkable disturbances at Brook House, and on October 23rd sent a manuscript to Stead which contained extracts from his diary.

Hastings' knowledge of the haunting began with his first visit to the house in the summer of 1873. The house was a squarish red brick structure faced by a court and circled by a high wall which obscured the lower-floor windows. When Mr. Hastings approached the building, he looked up at a second-story window and saw the figure of his friend, Miss B., grooming her hair and looking at him. A few days later, Miss B., upon inquiry, told him that he had seen something not normal and that the house was the scene of unnatural happenings.

Mr. Hastings asked to see the room where he had seen the apparent phantom peering at him, and they both walked to the "haunted room." After about ten minutes of studying the room and engaging in general conversation, they heard a strange sound of crashing bells for about thirty seconds. Mr. Hastings wrote that with this incident he had enough of the haunted room for the day and left. This, then, was his introduction to the incredible haunting of Brook House.

After this initial activity, poundings and noises of all kinds were heard, windows were opened and shut, chairs were tossed about, objects of all description were thrown through the air, voices were heard, and on one occasion, Miss B., who lived in the house with the other occupants, found that some of her hair had been burned away. This last incident reminds one of Bishop Pike's associate who, during the recent, odd incidents described in his book, *The Other Side*, found that her hair on more than one occasion had been singed.

During the haunting of Brook House, music, which seemed to the listener to have been a form of sad singing, occurred. This manifestation, the sounds of music, is a form of psychism which is extremely interesting and has been explored in a pioneering work by D. Scott Rogo in *NAD—A Study of Some Unusual "Other-World" Experiences* (University Books, 1970).

Apparitions were frequently seen, some of a most objective nature. On one occasion, a phantasmic figure resembling Miss B.'s dead sister was seen. The phantom was seen looking out of a window and, as the onlooker watched, it shut the open window.

On another occasion, the figure of a "fine tall woman" was seen walking to and fro holding a small child. With this phantom a very physical action was also observed when it extended a hand and the onlookers saw a "right-hand curtain wrenched away."

Perhaps the strangest-behaving apparition was described when the narrator wrote that, during one sighting, a white phantom showed itself at a window, bowed toward the viewers, and then seized a chair and threw it from the window. After this thoroughly objective act, it danced "madly" around the room and finally seated itself in a chair.

The account of this strange and fascinating case should be read. As I have mentioned, it can be found in William Stead's *More Ghost Stories*, which has been reissued by University Books.

As an afterthought to this case of haunting, a report entitled "Report of a Visit to Brook House, Fromley," by Lord Charles Hope and Mrs. Frank Heywood is included in the May–June, 1949, *Journal*, S.P.R. and gives statements from Mrs. Eliot and her daughter, who occupied the house. Both admitted hearing mysterious footsteps. A statement was also received from Mr. Michael Ackroyd, who had heard heavy breathing coming from the foot of his bed while at Brook House, but when he investigated these odd sounds he could find no normal cause.

Perhaps one of the most, if not the most, noted hauntings in parapsychological history is the famed and often discussed case described by Miss "R. C. Morton" (Rose Despard) in the *Proceedings*: S.P.R., Vol. VIII. The case has since been correctly titled the Cheltenham Haunting. Briefly, Miss Despard and her sisters (and on occasion, others) saw a phantom which appeared as a tall woman dressed in somber black. The phantasm was definitely "immaterial," but it apparently disturbed dogs. It showed a certain awareness of its watchers and avoided being touched. Inasmuch as this case has been described so many times, this very brief account will do.

Apparitions have been seen in cases of hauntings or poltergeist-hauntings and have demonstrated, on occasion, objective characteristics. They also at times have shown awareness of their viewers and as such, in view of the over-all mosaic of psychism, can be considered conscious, independent entities. The old view that all apparitions are a kind of nonthinking psychic robot has been shown to be thoroughly incorrect.

CHAPTER NINE

THE TWEEDALE PHENOMENA

THE REVEREND Charles L. Tweedale was a well-known investigator of matters psychical, a noted amateur astronomer, a man of many scientific interests, and the designer and maker of violins of great quality. He authored the noted books, *Man's Survival After Death*, *Present-Day Spirit Phenomena and the Churches*, *News from the Next World*, and other works. He investigated the mediumships of Mrs. Etta Wriedt, William Hope, and many others and personally experienced remarkable phenomena, which were credited to the extraordinarily powerful mediumship of his wife, Margaret.

Incredible psychical phenomena occurred at Weston Vicarage. They were chronicled by the Reverend Tweedale, and these effects ran almost the entire gamut of psychism. The "haunting," as it has sometimes been termed, represented in large part the apparent influence of the great violin maker, Antonio Stradivari, and other communicators, including his aunt, Elizabeth Coates. Tweedale had experienced psychical phenomena of a spontaneous nature when serving a curacy at Harrogate, and therefore was no stranger to such happenings.

The phenomena were well witnessed and Mr. W. W. Baggally, one of the famed investigators associated with the

Society for Psychical Research, who visited the "haunted" vicarage on a number of occasions, was extremely interested in the case. Twice he stayed with the Tweedales for several weeks and, considering that the phenomena which occurred were authentic, signed a statement to this effect in the Reverend Tweedale's diary.

Man's Survival After Death should be consulted for particulars regarding the phenomena encountered by the Tweedales and also *News from the Next World*, which is an extraordinary work filled with details of their experiences. This last work is unfortunately practically unavailable. At first sight it may seem completely extravagant, but it must be recalled that the manifestations described were well witnessed many times.

Today the entire field of psychism is at an extremely low ebb, and the parapsychological emphasis unfortunately has been placed almost entirely on statistical studies of ESP effects. As a result, most parapsychologists have little conception of the reality of objective psychical phenomena and cannot think beyond the narrow limitations of statistical studies. In my opinion, therefore, psychical research is in a period of great stagnation, but luckily there are a few hopeful signs on the parapsychological horizon—a very few investigators have personally witnessed poltergeist phenomena and have made statements to this effect. With these admissions, hope still exists. I submit that until objective, observable psychical phenomena are studied and not merely *inferred* ESP effects via statistics, parapsychology will continue to remain hopelessly becalmed and regressive.

I was very much amused and pleased to note that in the May–June, 1971, issue of the *Parapsychology Review*, in the

article headed "Parapsychology in Relation to Religion," Sir
Alister Hardy raises the question whether or not statistically
revealed ESP is really psychical. He points out that he does
not consider telepathy tests involving card-guessing particularly important, and voices the suspicion that inasmuch as
the chance results of various ESP phenomena, telepathy, pre-
cognition, psychokinesis (I prefer the term telekinesis; I feel
that it is a far more descriptive and accurate term) are so
much alike that perhaps they are in truth indicating something far different. The author notes that Spencer Brown, for
example, preferred to believe that these statistical results are
in reality demonstrating odd facts about the action of ran-
domness. And this is a far cry from telepathy!

Quite a number of parapsychologists would drop in a minute their card playing, if they were fortunate enough to be
able to encounter and investigate a case of good physical mediumship or an active, lively haunting. However, it is not socially acceptable in the parapsychological parlor to admit
this, for to concede that the general ESP program has been
vastly overrated and has, in all probability, wound up in a
boring, oh so boring, blind alley, still would lead to ridicule
by others in the field and a possible loss of grants and in-
come. So the endless card-guessing and ceaseless variations
of tests with falling weights, and experiments with the mo-
tions of insects and microscopic creatures presumably displaying a minute deviation from chance, will go on and on to
the utter boredom of both experimenter and reader.

I have been sounding this trumpet for many years and I
dare say will have to continue my warning and plea for many
years to come. It is a consoling pleasure to find occasionally
that I am not alone in my position.

I do not, however, think that any really constructive change will come until good phenomena and good mediums, both "mental" and "physical," again become available. Unfortunately, the art of development has been nearly lost and, until it is regained and widely practiced, I fear that little will be forthcoming in the way of worthwhile psychism.

I will add that in a previous book, *Experiences of a Psychical Researcher* (University Books, 1971) I have included a set of instructions which I have verified personally. These tell exactly how to achieve psychical raps. I hope that they will encourage some to experiment, achieve results, and go on from there.

But now back to the Tweedale phenomena. Rather than give a detailed chronological list of manifestations, I will merely include a number of incidents which featured apparitional forms. These incidents do not by any means exhaust the available examples but will, at least, provide a number of sightings for the reader's interest.

The majority of the numerous apparitions were seen only by Mrs. Tweedale. However, many were witnessed by others. The fact that Mrs. Tweedale on many occasions in the presence of others was the only one to see the apparitions she described does not, in this case, negate their possible presence. At certain times, when she insisted that she had seen a phantom, objective phenomena also occurred which can certainly be considered verifying evidence of a kind.

One of the earlier manifestations which occurred in the vicarage at Weston took place in December, 1907. Mrs. Tweedale awoke feeling cold and felt a breeze on her cheek. She then saw a tall column of a white, milky light, which soon disappeared. The following year the same effect was repeated. During the night of November 8th, the Reverend Tweedale was awakened by his wife, who told him in alarm that the same manifestation was again taking place. The Reverend Tweedale immediately sat up in bed and saw before him a cloudlike form of luminosity, which he estimated to be about four feet in diameter. The form rose and apparently went through the ceiling.

Mrs. Tweedale, upon questioning, said that she had first seen an apparition of a man bordered with light and, when she saw this phantom, she awoke her husband. She also saw the cloud of light into which the apparition had dissolved and watched it, with her husband, rise to the ceiling and disappear. The Reverend Tweedale notes that with this incident he no longer could doubt his wife's assertions.

On another occasion Mrs. Tweedale described a phantasmic figure of a man which disappeared after giving her a communication that at the time was not understood. Twice, some hours later, Tweedale awoke to hear a loud knocking over his head and mentions that his small son also heard the strange noises. In this case verification, in a sense, was provided by the fact that accompanying sounds were heard.

Mrs. Tweedale frequently remarked that the phantom figures which she saw were thoroughly objective in that they moved objects and were felt.

Regarding confirmatory noises which the Reverend Tweedale and others also heard, he stated that he had heard, literally hundreds of times, abnormal sounds such as crockery placed on a stand being moved about.

Tweedale's mother also saw various types of apparitional appearances. On one occasion in 1910 she and Tweedale's daughter Marjorie saw, in a room designated as the Red

Room, a phantasmic hand holding a flower. The hand apparently presented the flower for their inspection, and then moved it back from sight. Soon afterward Mrs. Tweedale saw a phantom man in the bedroom. She ran from the room to the Red Room, and the mysterious hand thrust itself through the open door and tossed the flower into the room. With this incident, thoroughly objective phenomena followed the sighting of an apparitional hand and entire figure, which were collectively observed.

To jump ahead a number of years, in 1932 Mrs. Tweedale saw an apparition of her husband's father. She had never seen him prior to his death and had never seen, as the Reverend Tweedale describes it, a colored picture of him. He had, in fact, died years before the Reverend Tweedale met his wife. Included in a description of the phantom seen by Mrs. Tweedale were the details of a ring set with a large carbuncle, sleeve links enameled blue, and a massive golden watch chain with a distinctive pattern of twisted links. The day after the sighting of the phantom, the Reverend Tweedale opened up a safe which he kept locked and discovered the sleeve links, which were exactly as described, and found the carbuncle ring. The watch chain had been gone far before the Reverend Tweedale's marriage. With the finding of these articles, and the description of the chain, a form of verification of the apparition was provided.

A quite complex series of communications involving Mrs. Etta Wriedt, as well as Mrs. Tweedale, is given regarding a small girl named Tabitha, who died many years ago as the result of a fire. This incident took place in the home of a friend of Mrs. Tweedale when she was present. Apparitions of the little girl began to appear in the early 1900's and were seen by all members of the family and the servants.

The Reverend Tweedale wrote that he had personally seen the apparitional form of Tabitha twice. The first time he saw her was in 1911 and occurred when he was passing the open door of the breakfast room. He saw a small girl by a table and at first sight thought that she was one of his daughters. He walked into the room, and the figure of the child immediately disappeared. At this time his wife entered the room and spontaneously remarked that she saw the little girl in the room. The Reverend Tweedale carefully notes that he had not said a word to his wife before she independently saw the apparition, and he also commented that his own children were outside the house at the time of the incident.

On another occasion, the Reverend Tweedale's wife saw an apparition of the little girl enter their bedroom and also saw her reflection in a mirror. This time, only Mrs. Tweedale saw the phantom.

In 1913 the Reverend Tweedale was sitting in a room reading a paper when he realized that a face had briefly appeared at the top of his newspaper and then had bent down out of view. He very naturally thought that it was one of his daughters but, after searching the room and finding no one, realized that it was an apparition. He sat down again to finish reading his paper. His wife then came into the room and spontaneously remarked that she saw the little girl there.

As noted in Chapter Four, animal apparitions were frequently seen by the Tweedales and, on occasion, were collectively sighted. One phantasmic cat, incidentally, did not represent a previous pet but was related to "Stradivarius," whose communications and apparitional appearances played a major role in the "haunting."

I must record a most strange manifestation at this point which, though strictly speaking does not belong here, is of great interest. The passage of matter through matter, the arrival of objects through physical barriers such as doors and walls, frequently was encountered by the Tweedales. Perhaps the most fantastic occurrence of this order happened after the Reverend Tweedale had performed a burial service for a man who had committed suicide. This, of course, is contrary to strict dogma. After the service had been said, Tweedale returned to the church and was entering the necessary details in the register when a large drop of blood appeared on the back of his hand. He quickly went outside the church and showed this incredible phenomenon to three men at the graveside.

This abnormal appearance of blood is not unknown to psychical history, and that is referring to blood phenomena other than with stigmatization. It has been noted by other investigators in matters parapsychological. Mrs. Helen C. Lambert, author of *A General Survey of Psychical Phenomena* (The Knickerbocker Press, 1928), friend of Dr. James Hyslop and assistant to Dr. Titus Bull, famed for his work with the phenomena of "obsession," personally observed the spontaneous production of blood at her home on three different occasions. These events were undoubtedly related to the presence of Mr. William Hannegan, who possessed great mediumistic abilities.

On one occasion blood appeared in profusion on the medium's hands, and Mrs. Lambert took them within her own and found them very sticky and wet. In fact, upon examination, the medium's hands and arms were found to be covered with blood but, in spite of its profusion and the fact that Mrs. Lambert had taken his hands in hers, no blood could be found on her hands.

A second incident took place when again Mrs. Lambert caught Hannegan's hand in hers. In this case her hand was covered with blood, which in turn left only a very faint trace on the medium's hand.

A third incident featured a far more startling effect, when blood was discovered streaming down the door of a cabinet which was locked. When the key was obtained from Mrs. Lambert's jewel box and the door opened, it was found that blood was also running down the inside surface of the cabinet door.

Professor Hyslop was extremely interested in these three incidents and in the *Proceedings*: A.S.P.R., 1908, Vol. II, expressed the preference for an explanation based on hallucinatory experiences. However, about a month after the *Proceedings* had been sent to press, he wrote to Mrs. Lambert admitting that his "mental theory" for physical phenomena would probably have to be discarded.

Interestingly, Dr. Gustave Geley wrote a letter to Mrs. Lambert telling how he had seen a stain of blood placed on the surface of a photograph of a murdered person. This letter is reproduced in Mrs. Lambert's book and was dated April 1, 1924.

I have seen another reference to the mysterious appearance of blood in a *Journal* of the S.P.R. but at the moment cannot find it to include with these other reports.

A most remarkable incident, including the vision of two apparitional figures of Sir Arthur Conan Doyle and Dr.

Bruce Low on October 10, 1936, is detailed by the Reverend Tweedale.

Tweedale had just awakened and was preparing to rise for the morning when he heard by the side of his bed and on the floor a resounding blow. He quickly left his bed but could find nothing amiss, and at that moment heard his wife outside his door saying that something remarkable had happened. When he had opened his door, his wife said that she had "awakened" from a strange vision. She had seen Dr. Low and Sir Arthur together and Sir Arthur had told her that for her benefit she should take potassium and iodine. At that point Sir Arthur put his hand to the side of her head. Upon inspection she found that a most peculiar mark was to be seen.

The Reverend Tweedale looked and saw heavily impressed marks of fingers on her temple, which were of a red-brown color. Mrs. Tweedale called to her daughters Sylvia and Dorothy to look, and they also saw the deep imprints on her temple. Actual skin markings could at first be seen by the Reverend Tweedale and his daughters, but this effect gradually faded away, and he very carefully notes that the finger markings were of a different shape than were his wife's. The finger impressions had square tips and, upon inquiry, Lady Doyle told Tweedale that her husband's fingers were square at the tips. Eventually, the unusual markings wore off but, before they had disappeared, the Reverend Tweedale photographed them to prove that they had actually been there.

With this strange incident, physical confirmation of apparitional forms, even though dreamed, was provided in a sense by the appearance of these impressions. It can be claimed that the markings were the product of a psychophysical mechanism, and this "explanation" could be seriously considered if it were not for the fact that frequent physical phenomena centered on Mrs. Tweedale. The incident does remind one of the odd markings which were seen on the skin of Eleanore Zugun, the "poltergeist medium." The possibility that the markings on the side of Mrs. Tweedale's head were produced by some psychological process exists, of course, but, when viewing the profusion of physical phenomena which centered on her, this explanation does not seem adequate.

An entire series of sightings of an apparitional cat is given in Chapter 5 of *News from the Next World.* The Reverend Tweedale, as well as other members of his family, saw these phantasmic cats, and this entire series of sightings presents an extremely formidable case for animal survival. In my previous work, *Animal Ghosts*, I have outlined these incidents.

Another group of sightings featured the appearance of a large black cat, which was seen by the Reverend Tweedale and his family and servants. In this case the phantom animal was associated with the apparitional appearances and subsequent communications of "Stradivarius."

The entire Tweedale phenomena provide evidence of a most interesting order, which can only be interpreted in terms of surviving spirits.

CHAPTER TEN

DEATHBED

APPARITIONS

THREE names automatically stand out when this subject is approached: Sir William Barrett, who wrote *Deathbed Visions*, published in 1926; Professor James Hyslop, who wrote to some extent on deathbed visions, including a chapter called "Visions of the Dying" in his *Psychical Research and the Resurrection*, material included in Chapter XII of *Contact with the Other World*, a paper in the *Journal*: A.S.P.R., Oct., 1918, also titled, "Visions of the Dying"; and Dr. Karlis Osis, who authored *Deathbed Observations by Physicians and Nurses* (Parapsychology Foundation, 1961). Many other writers have published material referring to deathbed phenomena, including J. Arthur Hill.

Sir William Barrett published a number of cases in his book which described incidents where the dying apparently saw dead relatives or friends who came to greet them and aid them at the time of death. He rightly observed that cases of this sort directly implied survival of death, and should be the subject of intensive study and investigation.

Professor Hyslop insisted on the importance of cases of this type and called upon his readers to report any such cases so that a record could be made. He further remarked that this inquiry should be extended to hospitals and asylums and hoped that physicians would also gather material of this order. Relative to the great importance of such cases, Hyslop wrote that, of the varied types of spontaneous psychical phenomena, only apparitions can provide evidence of survival. In both *Contact with the Other World* and *Psychical Research and the Resurrection*, a number of cases are given of visions of the dying, including a few examples taken from the very first edition of the *Journal* of the American Society for Psychical Research.

One particularly interesting case given by Professor Hyslop was originally recorded in Dr. Minot J. Savage's *Psychic Facts and Theories*. To outline this fascinating case: Two small girls about eight years of age lived in the same town. The two girls fell ill in June, 1889, and soon both died of diphtheria. Jennie died first and Edith was not told of her death. Unfortunately, she too could not recover and as she was dying she began to talk about other friends who were dead. From what she said, she appeared to see them. This could have been hallucination and, as Dr. Savage commented, to this point, nothing sensationally unusual had occurred. But suddenly she spoke to her father and remarked that she was going to take to the other world her friend Jennie. She then, in surprise, asked her father why he had not told her that Jennie had died. After these words, the dying girl welcomed her unseen friend.

Obviously, this type of case directly implies survival of death. An explanation of telepathy from the living who possessed the knowledge of Jennie's death can be advanced, but, as with other orders of survivalistic phenomena, the explanatory theory of survival, in this case, fits perfectly with the vast mosaic of phenomena which demonstrate that we do survive death.

Dr. Osis states in *Deathbed Observations by Physicians and Nurses* that more information about visions of the dying was highly desirable and therefore he had sent a questionnaire to 5,000 nurses and 5,000 physicians in order to discover their attitude and experience with this phenomenon. In the cases of favorable responses, telephone interviews and interviews by correspondence were undertaken. Dr. Osis sought primarily to explore visions of "hallucinations" of the dying and, in particular, "hallucinations of an apparitional nature," seen by a dying person who was properly aware of his surroundings. In short, interest was focused upon the experiences of a dying person when lucid and in full consciousness. Dr. Osis was also particularly interested in the moods of the dying: Why some die in fright and some die happy and elevated.

In summation, Dr. Osis states that certainty of results rests upon two primary features. One is that the belief of Professor Hyslop and Sir William Barrett has been confirmed: that dying persons who are in full possession of normal consciousness do "see" apparitions of the dead, of their friends and relatives who had died previously. And two, these "hallucinations" are of a phantasmic nature.

Consequently, in view of the finding of Dr. Osis and reviewing the findings and opinions of Hyslop, Barrett, and others, it can be firmly stated that the dying, on frequent occasions, see the dead. Sometimes they even see individuals whom they did not know were dead. And this phenomenon must be regarded as another facet of evidence favoring the survival theory.

An extremely interesting and valuable paper relative to visions of the dying is to be found in the *Journal*: S.P.R., September, 1959, titled, "The Grey Lady: A Study of a Psychic

Phenomenon in the Dying." It chronicles the records of nurses in a large London hospital which verified the recurrent stories prevalent at that hospital telling how a lady in gray comes to the aid of the dying. Accounts of six patients who did die are given which detail their encounter with the "lady in gray" who came to their assistance with the approach of death. Significantly, details of the apparitional figure matched and no discrepancies were discovered. The paper ends with the thought that the patients studied shared a psychical experience in that they saw an apparitional nurse dressed in gray who aided them during the advance of death. Again, this record of experiences of the dying can only suggest survival of death and direct intervention by the dead.

A very interesting example of an apparition of a mediumistic "guide," seen by a dying person, was recorded by Dr. Hodgson during experiments with Mrs. Piper. The narrator wrote that, when sitting with Mrs. Piper, he had been told by "Phinuit" that a near relative would die within six weeks or so. The sitter's wife was shortly afterward told privately by Mrs. Piper that her husband's father would soon die.

The writer's father did die soon, fulfilling the control's prediction. The dying man's daughter, it was discovered later, when sitting at the deathbed of her father, said that he had many times complained that an old man was present who discussed his private affairs. It must also be noted that just after the writer's father had died, "Dr. Phinuit," via Mrs. Piper, told him that he had attempted to influence the sick man relative to his will.

This entire case is particularly engrossing because it not only furnishes an example of a dying man who was aware of an apparitional figure who spoke to him, and matched statements by Mrs. Piper, who could not have normally known of this happening, but it has important bearing on the nature of Mrs. Piper's controls. If it should be considered that a telepathic exchange had taken place between Mrs. Piper and relayed through her control and the dying man, then at the very least a most interesting bit of paranormal action had taken place. However, the incident, in the light of the entire structure of survival phenomena, definitely suggests that her control, "Dr. Phinuit," did exist as an independent being. It does not matter if "Phinuit" furnished positive proof that he was who he claimed to have been. Actually, compared to the major point—was there an independent spirit there at all?— the question as to whether he was a French doctor is comparatively unimportant. It must be remembered that his "character" was spotty in a sense. He was prone to "fishing" for information from sitters, and he made statements regarding his supposed life on earth which could not be substantiated— traits very common to many living people. If this control did do a bit of lying and engaged in other practices not so pristine pure, still such facts do not automatically prove that he was a secondary personality, a creation of Mrs. Piper's sub-conscious. The facts merely demonstrated that a false name may have been given by a possibly real surviving spirit who acted as the medium's control.

In the chapter, "Visions of the Dying," from *Psychical Research and the Resurrection*, Hyslop presents a narrative which, though not strictly verifiable, is still worthy of serious consideration. The case again provides material suggesting the perception of an apparition of a mediumistic control by a dying person. Essentially, the narrator had a friend, a medium, whose control was called "Bright Eyes" (a typical-mediumistic name). The medium told the narrator, whose young son was ill with cancer, that the control would be with the child. During the night before he died, he complainingly remarked that a small girl was about his bed and, a few minutes before his death, the child said he believed that "they" had come for him. The boy's mother stated that he had not been told that the medium's control had promised to be with him.

The case was not presented by Hyslop as an evidential example of paranormal action, but he did believe that it fell into a common pattern of apparitional forms seen by the dying and was suggestive of the independence of a mediumistic control.

It might be thought by some that such visions seen by the dying should not really be called apparitions, but it must be remembered that, even if an apparent phantasmic figure is seen which is known to be the product of hallucination, still to the viewer it exists visually and as such is correctly termed an apparition. Apparitions can be placed on a scale which extends from the collectively seen, and even semiobjective, to apparitions which are pure hallucinations, devoid of any reality whatsoever.

In cases of dying persons, visions of relatives or friends who had died previously are comparatively common and can fit either into a pattern of telepathic activity or can be included in the great mosaic of general survival phenomena. I believe that all evidence now available points directly to survival.

An experience directly related to deathbed visions, though

in this case not by the dying, was included in the *Journal* of the S.P.R. by Dr. Hodgson. It was originally reported to Dr. Hodgson in 1902 by Dr. Burgers.

Briefly, Mr. G. stepped to the doorway in the room in which his wife was dying and, to his astonishment, saw three cloudlike forms suspended in strata in the air passing through the open doorway. Each form was about four feet long and six to eight inches wide. As Mr. G. watched, the three clouds floated to the dying woman's bed and veiled it in a mistlike shroud. Mr. G. suddenly saw at his wife's head a beautiful, miniature figure of a woman apparently shining with a golden luster. This form was dressed in a garment Grecian in style, and waited quietly with its hands lifted over Mr. G.'s dying wife. Two other figures were also seen, but as through a mist. Above Mr. G.'s wife appeared a duplicate body connected to her physical body by a cord which entered her forehead. As he watched this strange scene, the floating, duplicate figure at times shrank in size, and, when it did, it underwent a convulsive struggle. This procedure took place many times and Mr. G. watched this apparitional activity for five hours. Finally, his wife died and, as she did, the cord connecting the duplicate body to her physical body parted, and the double disappeared from view.

It was noted in the original report that Mr. G. was antagonistic to spiritualistic thought, and the physician who was caring for his wife signed a paper stating that Mr. G. was in no way prone to mental illness.

The appearance of the three cloudy forms over the body of the dying woman immediately brings to mind the curious misty spheres photographed by Dr. Baraduc at the death of his wife. The interesting fact that both descriptions are so very similar lends a certain degree of evidential value to each case, and, in spite of the criticisms leveled at Dr. Baraduc's "techniques of investigation," it is very plain to see that his accounts must be given serious consideration.

I will close this chapter with one last example of a deathbed apparition combined with a mediumistic communication which, when added to other types of survivalistic phenomena, presents an extremely strong argument for survival of death. This incident will be found in Dr. Hodgson's second report of his work with Mrs. Piper.

A "communicator," whom Dr. Hodgson designated Madame Eliza, remarked via the entranced Mrs. Piper that "she" had gone to the bedside of a certain dying man, had communicated a message consisting of an unusual choice of words, and had been seen. It was later discovered that two relatives who had been present at the bedside of the dying man had heard him state the very words which had later been reported by Mrs. Piper, and stated that he had remarked that he had seen an apparition of Madame Eliza.

A case of this type, not only provides a deathbed apparition but a concordant mediumistic communication and, as such, a most interesting and significant form of survival evidence.

CHAPTER ELEVEN

APPARITIONS

AND ASTRAL

PROJECTION

PHANTASMS of the living, to use the appropriate title of the pioneering work done by Edmund Gurney, F. W. H. Myers, and Frank Podmore, is simply another name for what is now known as astral projection. Other terms for this phenomenon are bi-location, out-of-the-body experience, the double, or even ESP projection. Still other terms exist but they are either so archaic or so seldom used that it will serve no purpose to mention them.

It was noticed long ago that many apparitions represented living people, and a well-known tradition existed which alleges that a phantasmic figure of oneself could be "projected" to a recipient. *A Strange Story* by Bulwer-Lytton, mentioned earlier, was based upon this old tradition.

The lore of witchcraft includes material which is directly related to astral projection. Relative to this lore is a curious reference found in Chapter VII in *Remarkable Providences Illustrative of the Earlier Days of American Colonisation* by Increase Mather, to the effect that appearances of living persons had been seen when it was later known that the originals were at home. Mather, however, wrote that such strange duplications were actually appearances created by demons.

A rule-of-thumb definition of astral projection is the extrusion of consciousness from the physical body. The consciousness is usually embodied in a duplicate body and, at times, is capable of leaving the immediate vicinity of the projector and is, on occasion, capable of bringing back memories of its travels. Cases exist where this information has been found to be correct even though it could not have been known normally to the projector. Cases also exist where the projector has been seen as an apparitional form.

Quite a number of books have been written about this subject, and some of the main works which bear upon this field will be listed below.

First, the remarkable and extraordinarily valuable series of works by Dr. Robert Crookall:

> *The Study and Practice of Astral Projection*
> *More Astral Projections*
> *The Techniques of Astral Projection*
> *The Supreme Adventure*
> *Intimations of Immortality*
> *During Sleep: The Possibility of "Co-operation"*
> *The Next World—and the Next*
> *Events on the Threshold of the After-Life*
> *The Mechanisms of Astral Projection*
> *The Jung-Jaffé View of Out-of-the-Body Experiences*
> *Out-of-the-Body Experiences: A Fourth Analysis*
> *The Interpretation of Cosmic and Mystical Experiences*

A general list of works devoted to this subject includes:

> *The Projection of the Astral Body*, Hereward Carrington and Sylvan Muldoon
> *The Phenomena of Astral Projection*, Muldoon and Carrington
> *The Case for Astral Projection*, Muldoon
> *Astral Projection*, Oliver Fox

The Mystery of the Human Double, Ralph Shirley
Practical Astral Projection, "Yram"
Man Outside Himself, H. F. Prevost Battersby
Out-of-the-Body Experiences, Celia Green
NAD—A Study of Some Unusual Other-World Experiences, Rogo

In addition, *Proceedings*: S.P.R., May, 1956, "Six Theories About Apparitions," by Hornell Hart. This study contains information vital to an understanding of astral projection phenomena based upon recent findings. A later paper, "Scientific Survival Research," which extends his findings, appears in *The International Journal of Parapsychology*, March, 1967.

Certainly one of the first things discovered about apparitions was their frequency about the time of death and during times of sickness and accidents.

In *Phantasms of the Living* (222), a case is given describing an apparitional experience which occurred to a barrister. He was sitting at his desk working when he found himself looking at a window pane, and there he saw the face and head of his wife with her eyes closed, her face white, and resting in a reclining position.

When he arrived at his home after working hours, his wife spontaneously told him that she had seen a young niece fall and cut herself and that she, in turn, fainted. Upon questioning, she said that this fainting incident must have occurred close to two o'clock, which was about the time when her apparition had been seen.

As with all such cases, a telepathic mechanism can be advanced, but it can be seen that the conditions for a projection resulting from shock were present. Interestingly, the fainting woman was wearing a dress which her husband had not seen before but saw correctly on the apparitional form.

Numerous apparitions are listed which include interior scenes of rooms, and picturizations of a dying person, including beds and surroundings, etc., which clearly cannot be attributed to a form of astral projection. In all probability, a telepathic process is involved at times plus the unconscious participation of the recipient in creating visions of this type.

Apparitions have been noted at the time of death which communicated the thought that the "originals" were dying at the moment that they were seen. However, in all probability, the appearance of some such phantoms actually occured immediately after death.

I have taken a related case from *Death and Its Mystery: At The Moment of Death* (pp. 341–43), which not only included a visual apparition which spoke, but provided an example of a death compact: an agreement to appear to the other after death. Two young girls promised each other that, at death, every effort would be made to appear to the living friend, kiss her, and say farewell. About five or six months later one of the girls woke during the night, saw her friend before her, and heard the apparition tell her farewell, that she was dying. The percipient's grandmother was in the room at the time the phantom was seen but saw nothing abnormal.

The girl went back to sleep but at a later hour again awoke to feel her friend kiss her forehead. Again she was told that her friend was dying. This last incident occurred at four o'clock in the morning. One hour later, an inquiry was made and it was found that her friend had died at four o'clock.

It is not actually made clear whether the apparition appeared during a dream or not, but in principle the last part of the case provides an apparitional warning of a death which took place after the original experience occurred.

Deliberately induced apparitions have long been discussed and are found in parapsychological literature. The often-noted case of deliberate projection by the wife of Mr. S. R. Wilmot is given in *Human Personality and Its Survival of Bodily Death* by Myers, which in turn was taken from the *Proceedings*: S.P.R., Vol. VII, p. 41.

Briefly, Mr. Wilmot, sailing from Liverpool to New York, dreamed one night that he saw the figure of his wife come into his stateroom dressed in a nightdress, hesitate, and then approach his side, bend down, and kiss him. After these actions the figure withdrew.

Upon waking, his fellow passenger who shared his stateroom remarked that a lady had visited Mr. Wilmot during the night. He was questioned and told what he had seen, which corresponded perfectly with Mr. Wilmot's dream experience. He repeated his description on three different occasions.

After Mr. Wilmot had landed and rejoined his family, his wife almost immediately asked him if he had seen her on the night that he had had his dream experience. She said that she had attempted to find him and crossed a violent sea to find a black ship. She then ascended its side, went into the ship, and found his stateroom. When she arrived at this point, she saw another man in the stateroom but went in and bent down to kiss her husband. It can be seen, then, that her description matched Mr. Wilmot's dream exactly.

This entire incident fits well into the pattern of astral projection and represents, I believe, an example of a deliberate attempt to see another person far removed by distance.

At this point I will offer a personal experience which provided a deliberately induced astral projection and subsequent sighting. I have mentioned this case in part in *The Enigma of the Poltergeist* and in some of my other works, but, due to its conformity to projections of this order, I will very briefly describe it again.

On February 5, 1955, I was seated on a couch at my home, when I saw a peculiar shadow form which was trapezoidal in shape and approximated the height of a man. It leaned at an angle to the right and seemed to have no connection with the floor. As I watched it in astonishment, it rushed—the only word I can really use to describe its strange motion—through two glass doors which were in an opened position and into the living room, where it suddenly disappeared. I automatically checked the clock and saw that it was 6:15 p.m.

I left my home and went about eleven miles to the studio of Mr. Attila von Szalay. When he met me at the door, I said, "Guess what happened to me." He replied that I had seen him and, in the course of the following conversation, stated that he had deliberately attempted to project himself to my home so I could prove to myself that astral projection was a reality.

There was no normal way that he could have known that I saw him—the strange trapezoidal apparition—and my remark, "Guess what happened to me" in no way could suggest what I had seen. The obvious answer to this incident is that a deliberately induced astral projection had resulted in the completion of Mr. von Szalay's plan to create a visible apparition of himself.

Another very well-known case of an induced projection employed the Reverend W. Stainton Moses as the percipient

or receiver. An account of the experimentally induced apparition was written by the "sender," and this account was cor-
roborated by Stainton Moses.

The agent wrote that one evening he decided to see if he
could appear before "Z." (Stainton Moses) but did not tell
him what he was planning. After retiring, he fell asleep in the
process of thinking about his potential viewer, and the following morning woke with no memory that an "astral excursion" had taken place.

A few days later he met Stainton Moses and asked him if
anything had occurred at his residence on the night designated for the experiment. The answer was an affirmative one.
The Reverend Moses said he was sitting before a fire
smoking his pipe when he suddenly saw the experimenter sitting in a chair close-by. As he watched, the figure faded from
view.

An example of an experimentally produced apparition,
perhaps even more well known, is the account furnished by
"S. H. B." given in *Phantasms of the Living*. The narrator first
began his experiments by attempting to will himself to be
present in spirit form in the bedroom of two young friends,
Miss L. S. V. and Miss E. C. V. He lived about three miles
from the prospective recipients of his trials.

On a particular Sunday evening S. H. B., on retiring to
bed, made this attempt, of course not mentioning in any way
his intentions to the two young ladies. He decided that the
time he would appear to his friends would be one o'clock in
the morning. The following Thursday he visited his friends,
and the older girl spontaneously said that close to one
o'clock in the morning both sisters had seen him standing
close-by.

S. H. B. wrote to Edmund Gurney on March 22, 1884, that he was going to make a similar experiment and attempt to journey in phantasmic form to his friend's house again. The time he picked to appear this time was twelve p.m.

A letter dated April 3rd was received by Mr. Gurney, which told how close to midnight she (Miss L. S. Verity) saw him appear within her room, and that he approached her and touched her hair. A confirmatory statement was included signed by Miss A. S. Verity, which said that her sister had told her that an apparition of S. H. B. had been seen which touched her hair, and that this account had been given her before S. H. B. had again visited them on April 2nd.

S. H. B.'s account of the incident stated that on Saturday, March 22nd, he made an attempt to project himself to Miss V. at midnight. He wrote that about ten days after this experiment he saw Miss V., who spontaneously remarked that she had seen him in her room on March 22nd at midnight, and that she had been so frightened that a doctor was called the following morning.

A case clearly related was described by the Reverend P. H. Newnham in *Phantasms of the Living* (Case 35) and tells how he dreamed that he was staying with the family of his future wife, saw her on a staircase, and rushed up to pass his arms under her arms and around her waist. This dream took place after he had fallen asleep after 9:00 p.m. The next morning he wrote to his fiancée describing this dream in detail.

The Reverend Newnham wrote that a letter "crossing" his and not answering it came from his future wife describing how at about ten o'clock in the evening, as she was going up a staircase to bed, she heard the sound of footsteps on the stairs and felt two arms passed around her waist.

Such cases, which should be read in their original form with full evidential detail, directly imply a form of astral projection. The Newnham case is included in Chapter V, titled "Specimens of the Various Types of Spontaneous Telepathy," and is listed as a hallucination which falls within the author's concept of telepathy. The intellectual climate of the Society for Psychical Research and society in general at this time was such that it was considered better to invoke theories of telepathy rather than exotic concepts of out-of-the-body experiences. However, in the light of today's knowledge of the phenomenon of astral projection and in particular the researches of Dr. Robert Crookall and Professor Hornell Hart, a far more probable and appropriate interpretation of these cases is projection.

A modern study, unfortunetely flawed, of induced "astral travel" is given in the *Journal*: A.S.P.R., January, 1968, by Charles T. Tart entitled *"A Psychophysiological Study of Out-of-the-Body Experiences in a Selected Subject."*

Dr. Tart met a young woman who reported that she frequently woke at night to find herself floating close to the ceiling in what seemed to her to have been a normal state of consciousness. These experiences lasted for brief periods of a few seconds to perhaps half a minute. She said that she had been having these experiences ever since she was a child and that they occurred several times a week. She also remarked that she had not made attempts to induce them deliberately.

Dr. Tart experimented with her in his sleep laboratory, and the technique employed involved the use of two rooms—one with a window so that the experimental subject could be observed. The subject slept in a bed in one room, and above her head about five and a half feet was a shelf on which was placed a piece of paper. The paper had written on it five random numbers which the subject was to attempt to read by floating from her body up to the shelf.

The first night of experimentation the subject reported that she had had no out-of-the-body experience.

The second night she reported that she had felt a floating sensation and asked that the time, 3:13 a.m., be written down. She had awakened at approximately 3:15 a.m., and Tart notes that this perhaps implied that she had floated above her body to where a clock, above the shelf, was located and had "read" the time.

The third night, Miss Z. reported that she had projected from her body several times but was unable to read the numbered paper.

The fourth night apparent success was achieved. She reported that she had floated from her body and had read the number, which was 25132. This number was correct.

Dr. Tart, assisted by Dr. Arthur Hastings, inspected the laboratory to see if theoretical possibilities of fraud existed, including the use of concealed mirrors, reaching rods concealed in her pajamas, and the possibility of reading the numbers from their reflection in the clock above the shelf. They discovered that by shining a flashlight on the number it was possible to read it, but Dr. Tart comments that this ability to read the number with augmented light represented an unlikely possibility. The sleeping room normally was dimly lit. Nevertheless, he notes that the reflection unseen in the dim lighting still represented a possible unconscious "stimulus." EEG readings were taken throughout the experiments but, in the present state of the art, I cannot see that their results can be reliably applied to these tests.

The entire experiment represented a splendid idea for the study of induced astral projections. It is unfortunate that proper precautions were not taken to eliminate the possibilities of fraud, conscious or unconscious. So, in spite of the experiment's possibilities, it remains a failure. I include it as a matter of interest only.

A very promising field exists with deliberately induced astral projections, and I am sure that, with continued experimentation, numerous successes will ensue.

Many good cases occur which provide evidence that persons who were ill or dying have spontaneously projected from their bodies to distant locations and have been seen in apparitional form.

The case of Mrs. John Goffe is a very old one indeed, but in spite of its age possesses good evidential value. Professor Hornell Hart thought it a sufficiently well-verified example to include in "Six Theories About Apparitions."

On the day before Mrs. Goffe's death at her parents' home on June 4, 1691, she intensely wished to see her two children, who were at her own home about nine miles distant. That morning, between one and two o'clock, she became entranced and after returning to consciousness insisted to her mother that she had visited her children at her distant home while she was sleeping.

The nurse who was taking care of Mrs. Goffe's children testified that she had seen an apparition of Mrs. Goffe leave the room where the oldest child slept to stand by the bedside where her youngest child slept with the nurse. She stated that she saw the phantom's mouth move but could hear no words, and when she attempted to speak to the apparition it moved away and subsequently disappeared. This incident took place shortly before two o'clock in the morning, and she became so very disturbed that at six o'clock she related her experience to neighbors.

So well known are apparitions seen before death that Flammarion, in *Death and Its Mystery: At the Moment of Death*, includes a chapter titled, "Apparitions before Death." From this chapter I took two examples of this phenomenon.

In Letter 46 the narrator tells how one morning she heard her maid walk into her parents' room. A few minutes later she saw the door of her room open and perceived her father. Thinking that he had come to tell her that her mother, who was ill, was worse, she asked him what he wished. Immediately the figure faded away. Her maid entered the room and, in answer to a question, replied that no one was ill. That evening the narrator's father had a stroke and died a little later.

Dr. C. J. Romanes contributed the following case, which was published originally in the *Proceedings*: S.P.R., Vol. XI. During the night Dr. Romanes believed that a door into his bedroom opened and he saw a white, phantasmic figure enter and stand at the foot of his bed. As it stood there, its viewer was able to see that its head and body were covered with white material appearing as veils. The phantom raised its hand and pulled back the covering over its face, and Dr. Romanes saw that the phantom bore the features of his sister, who was sick.

His sister died a few days later. The narrator wrote that his sister's illness had not been thought serious and her death had in no way been anticipated.

An apparition appearing as did this one seemed almost symbolic in its appearance and its behavior. Flammarion notes that it can be theorized that the invalid might have realized subconsciously that she was to die, and brought about in her brother's mind this effect. A telepathic process was advanced with this suggestion.

Professor Flammarion also proposed that Dr. Romanes' ill sister did, in reality, project from her body and was seen visually by him. Certainly the conditions for projection were present in that illness was present, a condition very conducive to astral projection.

Sylvan Muldoon, who discussed many of his experiences with astral projection in his book, significantly wrote that projection is far more frequent when bodily vigor is lessened and stated in the introduction to *The Phenomena of Astral Projection* that projections have been accomplished when the subject was in a state of coma or under an anaesthetic. The relationship of such projections to projections which have taken place when the subject was ill or dying is very clear. Without detailing the case, I have a friend who, I am convinced, is a "chronic" projector and experienced a projection when under the influence of sodium pentathol.

A number of cases of astral projection resulting in either objective phenomena or visible apparitions can be found scattered throughout parapsychological literature, and several examples are given in Dr. Robert Crookall's works. These cases are not evidential in the sense that they are accompanied by verifying material, but this does not argue against their reality. Dr. Crookall's extraordinarily important discoveries are based upon charting characteristics previously unknown, which could not have been anticipated. (The proof of this is that they had not been previously mentioned.) These characteristics are, in turn, based upon a study of a vast number of accounts of astral projection which are consistent with each other and follow definite patterns. It is true that, out of a large number of accounts of projection, some may be faulty, but if they are consistent with each other and reveal characteristics previously unknown, then each individual case must be granted serious consideration.

In *More Astral Projections* (Aquarian Press, 1964, Case 167) an account is provided by Mrs. Rosemary Buddle, well known and respected by Dr. Crookall, who tells how she woke during the night and saw what she first thought was her mother walking by the foot of the bed. She asked if "she" were all right, but no answer was received. She then by chance looked at the bed and saw her mother sleeping there quite normally. The phenomenon described in this case can only be interpreted as an extruded astral double. Again, I must remind the reader that, in spite of the absence of verifying material, such cases must be accorded consideration.

Another case very similar is also included in *More Astral Projections* (Case 205) in which Mr. E. G. Murray reports an experience wherein he, having fallen asleep, walked into his mother's room, passing through two doors en route. He found her sitting up quite awake in bed suffering from a migraine headache. He put his hands to her head and told her that it was two o'clock in the morning and that she should not be awake. After this remark, she thanked him and put her head down on her pillow.

The following morning, Mr. Murray's mother remarked that it had been very kind of him to look in at her, but she wondered why he had been up at two o'clock.

This example is again typical of a class of accounts describing projections resulting in apparitional form.

A particularly interesting case was described by Mr. Walter E. McBride, who stated that during the day of December 23, 1935, he was plagued by the thought that his father was possibly ill. After he went to bed he reported that he discovered that he was floating in a white illumination (Crookall's "vehicle of vitality"), saw his own body in bed, and then journeyed to his father's house. Arriving there, he found himself standing at the foot of his father's bed and saw his father looking at him in surprise. He then returned to his physical body and normal consciousness. It should also be mentioned that during his experience he was aware of an accompanying presence, which he later believed to have been a "spirit guide."

He immediately made a written record of his experience and, after two days had passed, saw his father, who lived a few miles away, and found that his father verified seeing him standing by his bed. The time of his father's "vision" matched the time noted previously by Mr. McBride.

This interesting case is also given in "Six Theories About Apparitions."

The evidence for the existence of astral projection at present consists of three main types. One lies in the vast collection of cases reported by those who have undergone the experience. The second is represented by the researches of Dr. Robert Crookall. The third category of evidence rests in the analysis of astral projections and apparitions of the dead given in Professor Hart's "Six Theories About Apparitions," which reveal that both phenomena are alike in general. A section of this report appearing in the *Proceedings*: S.P.R., May, 1956, states decisively that the hypothesis that phantasms of the living and of the dead are basically alike is verified by data collected.

There exist collections very large in extent of reported cases of astral projection by those who have either experienced the phenomenon themselves or who have seen projection apparitions. Sylvan Muldoon and Hereward Carrington in their second book, *The Phenomena of Astral Projection*, presented approximately one hundred cases. They vary, naturally, in value, and some are clearly of far less worth than are others. A following book, *The Case for Astral Projection*, by Muldoon alone provides another collection of cases.

The famed works, *Phantasms of the Living* and *Census of Hallucinations*, include a large number of cases which obviously fall into the category of astral projection. All verifying information is included in these collections.

The trilogy by Flammarion, *Death and Its Mystery: Before Death*, *At the Moment of Death*, and *After Death*, provides many examples of astral projection. Professor Flammarion comments several times that such cases demonstrate that the essential spirit of man is capable of leaving the body and communicating in one form or another—by raps and knockings and other physical phenomena including the strange stopping clocks, and in apparitional form—with a living relative or a friend. In the second book of his trilogy, *At the Moment of Death*, he notes that apparitions of the living occur in two main types: apparitions which are subjective and telepathic in origin, and phantasms which are demonstrably objective and nontelepathic. In the chapter, "Conclusions," in the last of his trilogy, *After Death*, Flammarion draws many important conclusions, including his belief that, as the time after death increases, the frequency of apparitions decreases; and his belief that apparitions can occur in "objective form," semiphysical in nature, and that we do survive death. Bearing in mind these principles, it is clear that apparitions of the living, astral projections, must share the same characteristics and do, of course, definitely exist, according to Flammarion's thought.

Again, I must mention that the majority of cases given in his works are of less evidential value in that verifying material seldom appears. However, Flammarion wrote that in many cases, he, for lack of space, left this accompanying evidence out. And it must also be remembered that in any collection of accounts, some examples, of necessity, were deliberately manufactured by correspondents, but this does not invalidate the vast majority. It should also be noted that the projection cases listed fall well within the pattern of such experiences and, in spite of extreme brevity at times, display the necessary characteristics charted by Dr. Crookall.

The American Society for Psychical Research and the Society for Psychical Research in England have published a steadily lengthening list of such cases.

In view of the truly immense amount of evidence now amassed, testifying to the reality of astral projection, it can very safely be regarded as factual.

CHAPTER TWELVE

QUESTIONABLE

APPARITIONS

AS IN all phases of the psychic, there are a great number of reports of apparitions and hauntings which have been the deliberate product of fraud. Various motives are behind these tales, including a desire for publicity; the wish for attention which, I believe, plays a major role in nonprofessional fraud; and the attempt to manufacture a psychical case so that it can receive publication in either books or magazines.

The history of psychical research has an abundance of such frauds and, needless to say, will continue to have them. In Chapter XII of *Haunted Houses*, Flammarion wrote that false hauntings are as numerous as genuine cases and that the very nature of the subject insures the prevalence of general fakery, hysterical mistakes, honest illusions and even hallucinations, and, most significantly, falsification by children.

This last, trickery by children, is a most important point. Children, it seems, take naturally and skillfully to manufacturing unreal hauntings. These "phenomena" generally consist of knockings, rappings, and tossed objects, but intermixed with these effects are marvelous stories of ghosts. I have investigated, of course, many cases of presumed hauntings. During the progress of these cases, ghosts were reported to have frequently stalked about, creating fear, awe, and publicity in quantity. And children were many times right in the midst of things working the effects both objective and verbal as was the Wizard when Dorothy, the Cowardly Lion, the Tin Woodsman, and the Scarecrow interviewed him in his throne room.

Adults are not angelic by comparison, it is quite true. Many have been the cases which I have studied which were pure invention, and children played no part in them. Perhaps the most complex and dramatic case of "haunting" that has ever been recorded was detailed in the *Proceedings:* A.S.P.R., Vol. I, Part 2, by Hereward Carrington. This report tells how a man who lived in a town in Nova Scotia was tricked by practically the entire town so that he believed that a vast haunting was taking place. Voices were heard, objects were tossed, knockings were heard, and, in short, a marvelous array of "psychism" occurred—all created by a group of townspeople in the spirit of a monstrous practical joke. And even an "apparition" of a headless man was seen by the victim of this "psychic" conspiracy. The case should be read by those who are interested in psychical fraud, for it is indeed a classic.

Another interesting case reported by Carrington is given in his book, *The Invisible World*. During this "poltergeist haunting," objects were tossed about and, at first glance, it did seem as if the poltergeist was at work. However, investigation soon revealed that a little girl, ten years of age, was the spirit behind the "phenomena." Carrington wrote that so proficient was the child in her psychical trickery that she had become near-professional in her use of fraud. A particularly interesting note was struck in this case, for Carrington treated the girl by suggestion when she was sleeping so that she would cease her practices. His treatment worked and the "haunting" ceased.

As remarked before, I have investigated a great number of reported hauntings, some including stories of visible phantoms flitting about the disturbed premises. One case in the San Fernando Valley, where for some odd reason many such tales originate, involved two girls, one about fourteen years old and the other sixteen or seventeen years of age. The parents were completely fooled by their children from what I could gather when I interviewed their mother, and, according to the stories told to me, visible spooks were flitting throughout the house at times. It soon became very apparent that the source of the "haunting" was the two girls, who had concocted a rather elaborate case over many months. At last, I intimated to the little conspirators that I did realize what they had been doing and that it would be better if they ceased their activities. Their reply led me to believe that the haunting would probably soon be a thing of the past.

Now and then one encounters those truly baffling cases which are a mixture of real and fancied phenomena. I studied at length a case in point which included marvelously active and actually destructive effects witnessed by a little girl and her grandmother. In this example, the grandmother, a most pleasant and kind person, witnessed many of the weird happenings alone, and I have no doubt that she did indeed see authentic poltergeist phenomena. The little girl, on the other hand, obviously had made up many of the manifestations which she claimed to have witnessed, and even long after the disturbance was over, told her grandmother that she had caused the entire affair. Without going into detail and having recourse to an elaborate analysis, I am sure that she too had actually witnessed genuine phenomena but had augmented the effects normally. The girl did have a most appropriate psychological "motive" for instigating the haunting, real and false.

Some few years ago, I became involved in an investigation of the haunting case which, upon analysis, gave all indications of lacking any paranormal elements. According to descriptions, an eerie, amorphous apparition was occasionally seen and other apparitional manifestations were encountered. Actually, the descriptions of the ghostly happenings were not divergent from a general pattern of genuine haunting effects, but I became convinced nevertheless that no real evidence was at hand which would lead me to believe that paranormal activities either had happened or would happen.

To my amazement, some years after, I was stunned to read a book which included an account of this case telling how I had actually seen a psychical manifestation occur (which I most certainly had not) and stating that I had gone into a trance and a "spirit" had proceeded to write messages through my hand. It goes without saying that these statements were totally false. After all, I am an investigator and do not act as a "medium." I could hardly believe what I saw in print before my eyes.

So, not only do "hauntings" which are nonparanormal exist, but publications print tales about investigations which are completely distorted. Unfortunately, I cannot find a suitable moral to draw from this tale to present in smooth, epigrammatic style, and must rest content with the bare recital of the facts.

False hauntings, printed distortions of cases, and published accounts which have no element of truth in them whatsoever are not confined to our contemporary years but will be found in earlier literature fairly frequently. For example, an article entitled "The Journalist at Large in Psychical Research" is included in the *Journal: S.P.R.*, April, 1905, and offers a splended case of two examples of "psychism" which were the product of pure invention in one case and of distorted reporting in the other.

The first case mentioned in the article falls outside the subject matter of this book, but it is so illustrative of how "psychic" stories are frequently born that I thought it well to include it. The case is one which achieved notoriety in the early 1900's and which sported the title, "The Talking Baby of Bethesda." According to the stories which were passed about, a baby in Wales died at the age of three months but, before its death, prophesied that woe and disaster would be the lot of the following year—1904. It is also mentioned in the article that this tale, modified in form, popped up in connection with that remarkable and thoroughly interesting phenomenon, the famed Welsh Revival. I will note, at this point, that this movement did actually feature genuine paranormal lights and perhaps other effects which formed the basis for certain of Arthur Machen's beautiful writings.

The solution of the talking baby mystery was very simple. A reporter, looking for sensational copy, met a brother journalist and asked if anything exciting had happened worthy of print. He was then jokingly told of the incredible baby prophet and, after jotting down the details of this miracle which was invented on the spot, dashed off to telegraph the wild tale back to his newspaper. After the story had been launched on its career of crime, the reporter who originally invented the story professed to have been amazed that it had received serious consideration, but, in spite of telegraphed retractions, the story was still printed and went on to achieve fame and fortune.

The second example given in this short paper involved an alleged haunting of a house in Brighton, where it was reported that an apparition of a transparent woman in a brown dress had been seen by three men. A story had been circulated previously that a young woman had hanged herself in this house, which, of course, well set the stage for a "haunting" legend. An occupant of the house was interviewed who said that he had not seen the ghost but that he and his wife had heard three notes struck on the strings of a guitar which was suspended on a wall.

With this material to go on, which was taken from newspaper accounts, the "case," to grace it with that title, was published in the *Annals of Psychic Science,* but it was printed so that it seemed to have been recently reported.

In the same issue of the *Journal,* a correspondent further discussed this haunting story. He was the original source of the account which had appeared in newspapers and stated that he had been approached by a reporter who wished to gain the details of his experiences in the disturbed house. The story was printed as though the incidents had recently occurred instead of fifteen years before, and did not give the name of the man who offered the original story. It is further noted that a journalistic touch was added which insisted that the young woman who had hanged herself in the house had done so because of cruel treatment by a man. She actually was forty-two years old when she committed suicide and was a lodging housekeeper who was staying in the house. There was no hint of cruel treatment.

Actually, considering the way stories of the supernormal, and, in fact, any story about practically anything today distort the original occurrence, these false touches are mild indeed.

For example, a few years ago I investigated a case in a small town about 150 miles from Los Angeles, called Porterville. The case featured a "phantom phone" in an old railway station which was being restored and rebuilt as a museum. According to the papers, a mysterious phone was frequently heard ringing but could never be traced to its source. Finally, Mr. Ceil Smith and I found that the ringing emanated from a very old phone on the outside wall of a lumberyard building in the vicinity. When the wind was exactly right, and it did shift from direction to direction constantly, the sound was carried into the empty rooms of the station, to there form a marvelous illusion of sound. It was an illusion in the sense that it sounded exactly as though it had come from an antique telephone and that, no matter what room one was standing in, it sounded as though the ring originated from the depths of another room. This effect was really quite startling, and it was not hard to see why it had been dubbed the "phantom phone."

When we had solved this odd little puzzle and presented our solution to a local newspaper, which printed it, we naturally assumed that the case of the phantom phone was dead and laid to rest.

Not so. To my surprise and disgust a few years later a newspaper featured a long, several-page article devoted to supposed "hauntings" and other dubious marvels, and lo, there I saw the phantom phone case in all its glory. As I read, it quickly became apparent that the author of this epic left the reader with the thought that the case had never been solved and that ghostly forces had been at play. Now it is obvious that the writer should logically have contacted the town's newspaper regarding the "haunting" (in the course of our investigation that was one of the first things that we did), and if this had been done it would have been quickly ascertained that no mystery remained and that the puzzle had been completely solved.

So it is with many cases of supposed hauntings and matters psychical. Frequently, thoroughly distorted versions are seen in print, with an occasional account correct in all or most detail, and I wonder at times how, outside of technical parapsychological literature (and at times even this can be faulty) anything is ever reported correctly.

Contrary to the rather dismal record in the last few years of so-called haunted houses, there have been completely validated cases of poltergeists which have been studied recently. Various manifestations, such as tossed objects, have been witnessed, and there is no dispute as to their reality. However, with the recent cases of poltergeist activity I am not, at the moment, familiar with any which have presented any evidence for apparitional activity

Occasionally one hears about "apparitional" figures which have appeared on television screens, on the surfaces of windows, etc. Periodically accounts are given in magazines and newspapers of odd figures, usually of a religious nature, which have been found on glass and are generally considered by their discoverers to be miraculous in origin. Figures have been reported as appearing on walls and even on leaves.

Most of these oddities can be safely attributed to perfectly normal causes. I have seen photographs of leafy "apparitions" and, while some are at first sight somewhat startling, it is obvious that they are simply chance configurations. The window pane "apparitions" many times are the result of the pasting of a picture on a window and the very normal transference of the image to the glass. Such "mysteries" are easily explained, even though they are curious and interesting.

Oddities have been seen on television screens, which again are due to perfectly normal processes. A case of a television "phantom" was published in the *Journal*: S.P.R., March, 1969, which, though presenting absolutely no evidence for paranormal phenomena, does furnish an interesting and illustrative oddity. The report was entitled, "A 'Ghost' on Television." It seems that in 1964 an English television program was devoted to a discussion of mediums, fortunetelling, phantoms, etc. An investigation of a reputedly haunted house was conducted to demonstrate to the viewers how such a study was accomplished.

While the investigation was in progress, the "investigator," who remarked that he had found no evidence for actual haunting phenomena as a result of his studies, stood before a large window. The room was illuminated by powerful arc lights, since it was very early in the morning and quite dark outside the house.

Eventually, twenty-seven viewers wrote in reports which told how they had seen mysterious effects on their screens. Of these accounts, fifteen wrote that they had seen the form of the priestly figure or monk. Two believed that they had seen figurations which fell outside this general classification. Variations were found in many of the accounts, and seven of the writers expressed their belief that the figure seen was actually an illusion.

Included in the article are two photographs which represent the incidents when they took place, and two drawings are provided which show where the supposed apparitional figures are located. Careful examination will reveal to the critical viewer, I am sure, that absolutely no spectral figures can be seen. And I am also sure that the credulous will, in all seriousness, maintain that ghostly figures will be found in the photographs.

This willingness to imagine ghostly phenomena is, of course, the bane of psychical science, and, if one wishes to experience this depressing fact in all its full splendor, may I suggest that a common, garden variety professional materialization séance be attended. I will guarantee that it will be replete with affirmations that the "spooks" (the medium or helpers in costume) are dead relatives and friends, and that any mistake of identity is absolutely impossible.

CHAPTER THIRTEEN

APPARITIONS IN EARLIER years, and even in years not too far removed,
SHOWING apparitions have been generally considered as a kind of
INTELLIGENCE psychical robot, a mindless automaton, which fit into the
AND AWARENESS generally prevailing attitude of antagonism toward the concept of survival of death. In fact, undoubtedly a large number of parapsychologists would, if questioned today, maintain that apparitions are the product of a telepathic process, have no objective qualities, and are limited in their apparent actions to the degree that they possess no independence from either agent or percipient and have, of course, no self-awareness or awareness of onlookers.

In the introduction to *Phantasms of the Living*, primary theses are given and one, the third, states that apparitions demonstrate that "supersensory" activity between minds exists. Telepathy, then, is implied. In that same introduction Mrs. Sidgwick, far predating Gardner Murphy, wrote that with an apparently objective hallucination of a person in the process of dying, an apparition, the primary element transferred from the agent to the viewer, is generally the mere idea of the dying sender's personality. The rest, such as clothing, is supplied by the receiver's mind. With this concept, the apparition is granted no independent existence—most certainly no element of objectivity—and no awareness of self or viewers. In other words, a psychically inspired, hallucinatory robot is postulated.

The prevailing view until quite recently was that, due to observations that apparitions usually are silent, their behavior was restricted to one apparent purpose, and are what can be described as automatic or semiautomatic in their action. Therefore it was felt that they must not be surviving spirits or conscious beings.

As an example of this view, Dr. Raynor C. Johnson, even though a survivalist, wrote in *The Imprisoned Splendour* that phantasms exhibit behavior of a semiautomatic order which seems to be limited to a single thought. He further stated that this lack in variety of behavior is greatly unlike the behavior of a living person.

G.N.M. Tyrrell, of course, regarded phantoms in the sense of a psychical robot and considered that their behavior could be considered part "volitional" and part in the nature of an automaton. In this vein, the apparition was not thought of as a carrier of consciousness.

Not all psychical researchers were satisfied with this general theory and, as mentioned earlier, F. W. H. Myers could not swallow this thought easily and occasionally expressed discomfort. It does seem to me that he really did think that certain phantoms were actually what they represented, that is, they were surviving spirits which on occasion did possess some form of objectivity.

Hereward Carrington, who earlier in his psychical career espoused spirit survival which, for example, he openly expressed in the last part of his book, *Eusapia Palladino and Her Phenomena*, published in 1909, did not completely accept the subjective theory of apparitions. In *The Story of Psychic Science* (1931), he wrote, in the section devoted to apparitions that a number of cases definitely indicated that something other than a telepathic exchange was at work and that an actual "astral body" was sensed.

At the end of his discussion about hauntings, he admitted that telepathic theories explained much about apparitional phenomena but not, necessarily, all. He wrote that, when reviewing the material indicating a semiobjective nature for some apparitions, he found that this evidence did argue for some form of objectivity.

I think that, like Myers, Carrington during the period when he finally abandoned the survival concept still was not completely settled in his mind regarding the nature of apparitions. When it is remembered that he co-authored *The Projection of the Astral Body* and *The Phenomena of Astral Projection*, which are devoted to the belief that we are, at times, capable of projecting a double from our physical body which, in turn, for all practical purposes, is synonymous with survival of death, it is hard to reconcile the thoughts expressed in these books with his stated conviction that we do not survive death. Naturally, this last opinion would certainly imply, at the very least, that apparitions are not capable of consciousness.

This, then, was the general view of the majority of parapsychologists until recently—apparitions are mere hallucinatory structures created by the minds of both the "sender" and the "viewer," and have no awareness of self or of others.

Of course, many exceptions could be found in the ranks of

psychical researchers. Frequently researchers who had, in the course of their investigations, the opportunity to witness major phenomena in quantity were survivalists and believed that phantoms were, at least at times, actual spirits and not mere "robots." Perhaps a general rule might be discovered: that with an increase in actual experience of genuine psychical phenomena and not inferred ESP phenomena, acceptance of survival and of conscious apparitions also increases.

Further discussion of apparitional theory will follow after a presentation of different classes of pertinent cases.

Perhaps the first type of apparitions that should be considered are those which spontaneously appear and in one way or another furnish information that they have died. Such action directly implies that they possess awareness of self and of others to some degree.

In *Death and Its Mystery: After Death*, Flammarion offers a case (Letter 4443), which describes how the narrator, during the night, heard a voice call his name several times. Later the same voice called again and the narrator, upon opening his eyes, saw an apparition of his friend by his bed. The phantom spoke, saying farewell and asking that his family be comforted.

The next morning the narrator went to his friend's home and found that he had disappeared. Eventually his body was found, and in his hand was grasped a bottle of cyanide in solution.

At first glance, according to the account, the apparition was obviously a conscious being attempting to carry out an intelligent and necessary action—that of aiding his family.

In *Phantasms of the Living* (Case 25), a case is offered of an apparition which clearly implies a conscious intent to convey news of death. The case is well documented and the original account should be read. An accident occurred between two ships. The captain of one, Captain Collyer, was killed when the mast of his ship apparently fell on him and split his head. When his body was found, approximately ten minutes after the two ships had collided, it was noted that his nightclothes were soiled and his face was badly marred.

Captain Collyer's mother, during the night of the accident, suddenly saw an apparition of her son standing in her bedroom gazing earnestly at her with his head bandaged, wearing a nightcap which appeared very dirty, and wearing soiled nightclothes. She also saw that his face was badly marred.

It can be safely concluded that Captain Collyer was killed instantly and therefore could not have foreseen that his head was to be bound up with a dirty cloth. This fact certainly argues that, if his apparition had presented itself in such a manner, "it" must have realized that the cloth had been placed on "its" head after death.

The authors of *Phantasms of the Living* plainly realized this implication and, in what I can only regard as an attempted evasion of this possibility, suggested that the original telepathic transmission to his mother carried the thought of death and that she, in turn, via a subconscious process, conjured up the bandage, etc., as a conventionalized picturization of death. This suggestion, I think, is very far fetched and cannot be applied to the incident as a counter-argument to a surviving spirit represented by the apparition.

A case similar, in that the apparition communicated the fact of its death, originally appeared in the *Journal*: S.P.R., May, 1908, and was used by Sir William Barrett in his book, *On the Threshold of the Unseen*. The case was first received by

Barrett from a friend whom he presented to the Society for Psychical Research, where she was thoroughly cross-examined for possible flaws in her testimony.

In the spring of 1907 a man in London committed suicide by shooting himself. On the day of his funeral, three days after his death, his apparition was seen by his godchild. During this appearance the phantom communicated to her the news of his death, the fact that it had been by shooting, and why he had done it. He asked that she pray for his benefit.

All news of the death was kept from his godchild until some days after the funeral had been held, and, in fact, all that was then said was that he had died. The girl returned to England from the convent on the continent where she had been staying, and her mother was astonished to hear from her the full details of the suicide, which had been conveyed by the apparition. As Barrett notes, a full investigation confirmed the fact that all information regarding the tragic death had been kept completely from her and there was no normal way in which she could have received this knowledge.

Again, with this case, a phantom is described which gave every indication of being an aware being, possessed by, certainly, partial consciousness of others, and fulfilling a deliberate plan—that of informing "its" viewer of death. The most obvious interpretation of such an incident is that a surviving spirit was represented.

From a paper, "A Series of Spontaneous Cases in the Tradition of Phantasms of the Living," *Journal*: A.S.P.R., July, 1951, an example of an apparition's reporting its own death was furnished by Mrs. Gladys Watson. After sleeping for some hours, she was awakened by a voice calling her name. She sat upright in her bed and saw her grandfather standing close-by. The phantom spoke, saying that she was not to be frightened and that "he" had just died. It continued to speak, saying that his body would be buried in a certain manner. The figure also remarked that "he" had been wanting to pass over since the death of his wife.

Subsequent investigation revealed that the narrator's grandfather had died that night, and her account was confirmed by her father.

Somewhat on the same order of apparitions which give evidence of their death either by communications, details of dress, or other indications, are cases which represent fulfilled compacts. These examples of phantasms appearing in discharge of promises to appear after death have occurred in some number, and many examples will be found throughout parapsychological literature. Again, at first glance, such behavior represents a being which is aware and deliberately carrying out a previous plan.

In the *Journal*: S.P.R., July, 1894, an account originally written by the percipient describes how, when with friends, she was ascending a staircase and suddenly saw the tall figure of a man standing nearby. Startled, she reached out and found that her hand passed through the figure. She stepped closer and then was able to recognize the apparition as that of a friend who was at the time in India. This incident occurred during the evening of December 6, 1892. Some days later she received the news that her friend had died on that same evening. Significantly, the writer stated that her friend had frequently insisted that, if he died, he would manage to apprise her of that fact. Complete verifying material accompanied this account.

In the *Journal*: S.P.R., September, 1885, is a very nice

specimen of a compact apparition (Case L 2325). The percipient spontaneous awoke from her sleep to see a phantasmic figure very near her bed holding up to her view a ring which had been previously given to the original of the apparition by the awakened sleeper. The figure stayed in view for several seconds and then faded from sight. The percipient was understandably frightened and, when morning came, related to her mother what had happened during the night. She stated that she believed her friend had died—in spite of having found her in good health just two weeks previously.

Eventually she received a letter which told of the death of her friend. Enclosed with it was the ring. The dying girl, the letter stated, had asked that the ring be sent back.

It must be remembered that, paralleling such apparitional phenomena, a great number of cases have been reported in which information relative to death has been received by other means. For example, many cases exist in which the percipient or percipients have received notification of death by hearing an apparent external voice. Cases of apparition must not be considered apart from examples which have also provided phenomena heralding death such as knocking, the traditional stopping of clocks, the fall of pictures from walls, the breaking of objects, and so forth. All must be considered as part of a great well-fitting mosaic of interlocking phenomena, each blending into the other and partaking of common elements.

A case in point is headed "Remarkable Experience of Miss Vaughn," and is included in the *Journal*: S.P.R., October, 1885. Miss Vaughn had a good friend who had been dying, and then seemed to recover. A daughter wrote to Miss Vaughn saying that they would like to come to London, which was twenty miles from their home, to see her if convenient.

One night, soon after she had received the letter, Miss Vaughn, while lying awake in bed, was surprised to hear three series of three extremely loud raps that sounded on a box which had been placed by her bed. She then heard a woman's drawn-out cry which, as she described it, faded away as though it had receded into the distance. Miss Vaughn called the maid, who had heard nothing. She asked the maid to note the time, which was ten minutes to one in the morning.

Later that same morning Miss Vaughn received a letter which stated that her friend had died during the night. Still later, she heard from the nurse who had attended her dying friend that she had died at fifteen minutes before one. The nurse further related that the dying woman had given a loud cry at the instant of her death.

I will mention that at the death of a member of my family I was awakened by the apparently objective sound of a great gong being struck. The sound was subjective in nature, inasmuch as no other member of my family heard the incredible and awesome sound.

Incidents of this general type are very common, and parapsychological literature is filled with cases offering such phenomena. The works of Professor Flammarion in particular are rich with similar accounts.

There is a large class of apparitions which have given various indications that they were aware of their viewers and consequently showed that they were, as Dr. Robert Crookall and Professor Hornell Hart express it, vehicles of consciousness.

Professor Flammarion in *Death and Its Mystery: After Death* (Chapter VI) published a case where the writer, Jules Lermina, saw an apparition of his cousin which gave every indication of being a conscious, intelligent being. The writer had left his dinner table, gone into the kitchen, leaned down to pick up a dish, a most prosaic action and far removed from the proper Gothic setting for the traditional, literary ghost, when he heard his name called by his cousin. The narrator looked up at the window and saw the form of his cousin, who nodded to him and greeted him, wishing him a pleasant day. Surprised, the narrator dashed upstairs and looked out into the street, but could see no one there.

His father, who was surprised to hear the front door opened without its bell being rung, was told that the narrator's cousin had appeared but must have hidden himself in a teasing mood. The father then told him that the cousin had died the day before but he had not wished to mention the sad news. The writer concludes with the note that he had, then, seen the apparition of a person who had died twenty-four hours before and had spoken to the phantom in a normal manner and had heard an equally normal-sounding reply.

A particularly interesting case included in the *Journal*: S.P.R., January, 1894 (G 244), offers a collectively seen apparition of a woman who communicated a long "message" which consisted of a warning to her living husband to cease from evil actions and told that if he did not alter his ways his soul would be in danger. The narrator, who was present at the time, stated that he was utterly convinced that the apparitional figure was that of his friend and that this conclusion was brought about by the phantom's telling him of an incident and a conversation which were known to no living person other than himself.

From Mrs. Sidgwick's *Phantasms of the Living* (G 275), a case reports a visible phantasm which, though giving no sign of noticing the two witnesses who were present during the incident, showed awareness and concern for a child. The phantom was seen to lean over a sick child and displayed, according to the report, a look filled with great affection. The apparition, which vanished after a short time, was recognized as the mother of the sick boy, who had died previously.

There is a class of apparitions which offers first-rate evidence that they are perfectly aware of their viewers, are clearly "vehicles of consciousness," and are imbued with a purpose to accomplish a desired end. Such examples obviously fall into the survival classification. In the interest of completeness, I will give one example.

Briefly, a Catholic priest was told by a woman by the name of Anne Simpson, who belonged to the Presbyterian Church, that a friend of hers had been troubled by the appearance of a female apparition named Maloy, who requested that a small debt be paid. An investigation was made by Father M'Kay, who discovered that the woman represented by the apparition had lived, had worked in a regimental laundry, and did owe a butcher a small sum of money. The debt was paid and Father M'Kay wrote that the apparitional visits then ceased.

The preceding case appears in *Human Personality and Its Survival of Bodily Death* (II, 348) by F. W. H. Myers, in Robert Dale Owen's *Footfalls on the Boundaries of Another World*, and in Flammarion's *Death and Its Mystery: After Death* (p. 79).

Phantoms which have been observed in cases of hauntings have frequently displayed some form of awareness of their onlookers.

The famed phantom seen in the Morton haunting described by Miss R. C. "Morton" (Rose Despard) did, on occasion, demonstrate a definite awareness of "her" viewers. On January 29, 1884, Miss Despard saw the phantasmic figure walk into a room and stand by a couch. Miss Despard approached the figure and asked aloud of she could be of any assistance. The phantom stirred and apparently attempted to speak, finally managing a gasping sound. After this effort, it left the room, went into a hallway, and vanished.

Miss Despard wrote that several times she tried to touch the ghostly figure but each time she made the attempt the phantom was "beyond" her. Miss Despard also wrote that, when the apparition was "trapped" in a corner, it evaded "capture" by vanishing.

On July 21st, she saw the phantom enter a room and approach the couch where she was sitting reading and then stand close-by. The apparition remained in this position for about a half hour. Finally it left and went to a door through which it passed to walk through a hallway and disappear at a garden door. Miss Despard again attempted to speak to the phantom woman but, in spite of the fact that the ghost stopped and apparently tried to answer, no words were said.

On occasion, Miss Despard saw the figure but others with her were not able to see it. However, the figure was seen by other witnesses, and there is no reason to doubt its existence. Footsteps and "noises" were heard frequently in the disturbed house and were clearly associated with the phantom.

Evidence does exist which indicates that dogs were in some

manner aware of the presence of the phantom, or at least aware of the presence of paranormal forces in the house.

As is very well known, Miss Despard became convinced that the figure was not constructed of a material substance. She now and then placed strings across the stairway steps and fastened them with little globs of glue so that the most minute touch would unfasten them. Twice she saw the phantom walk through the strings. In no way were they disturbed.

This case is of extreme interest and was originally published in the *Proceedings*: S.P.R., July, 1892.

The apparitional forms witnessed during the Tweedale "haunting" displayed, in every way, complete awareness of their viewers and, short of simply ignoring the case completely or adopting the desperate measure of denying that it occurred, the only possible interpretation of the phantasmic activity is an openly spiritistic one.

An intriguing case, appearing in the *Journal*: S.P.R., November, 1893 (G 242), featured a collectively seen apparition which really falls into the haunting category. A mysterious figure, which according to description was of a phantasmic nature, was occasionally seen on a road. However, for the purpose of illustrating the point that certain apparitions associated with hauntings have shown awareness of their viewers, I will give a brief account of two encounters with the apparition which frequented the area.

Two sisters were walking home one evening when they saw coming toward them a tall man dressed in black clothing whom they thought, at first sight, to be a clergyman. It strangely disappeared from sight but was again seen, though this time by only one of the girls. The other was unable to see any trace of it.

On the other occasion, one of the sisters was again walking on the same road at ten o'clock in the morning when she saw the phantom in front of her. She ran after the figure and finally overtook it. It suddenly stopped its "walk" and turned around to face the young lady. With admirable honesty she admitted that she was frightened and stopped her pursuit. The apparition, who was dressed in the same costume as before, peered at her with, as she described it, an empty look, and, as it did, she noticed that its color was abnormally pale.

The figure watched her for some moments, then moved several steps away and deliberately looked back at her. After this last action the figure performed that most traditional action of all self-respecting ghosts and faded away.

Clearly, the apparitional form seen in this case was perfectly aware of its viewer and reacted in a manner which revealed this awareness. How far its conscious level, to express it that way, approached normal awareness is another matter, but at the very least it did definitely demonstrate that it "perceived" its pursuer.

The very few cases which I have listed provide examples of haunting apparitions revealing a certain degree of awareness of their surroundings. Naturally, it is impossible to determine how extensive this awareness was, but there is valid reason to believe that it varies from limited, fixed attention to a simple or single purpose to a full, complex consciousness, perhaps little different from that which we experience during our waking hours.

The phenomenon of "astral projection," or, to use a contemporary parapsychological term which I personally hold to be very inexact and misleading, ESP projection, provides a rich mine of apparitional manifestations which are of utmost significance to the study of apparitions, as well as to the entire field of psychical research. I do think that a study of the various works devoted to astral projection is an absolute necessity for any real understanding of apparitional phenomena, and for an understanding of general psychism as a whole.

Even though the experiences of astral projectors such as Sylvan Muldoon and Oliver Fox, and I might add Ralph Shirley, are not evidential in themselves in that verifying material which would conform to very strict standards of evidence was not furnished, still there is an internal coherency and concordance with all accounts of this phenomenon, which demand the most serious consideration. Further, such reports display certain characteristics charted by Dr. Robert Crookall which were unknown before his discoveries. In other words, most of the worthwhile accounts of astral projection experiences include verifying internal evidence.

A study of these experiences will reveal many characteristics directly related to the nature of apparitions and in particular apparitions which, in their behavior, give evidence that they are, to one degree or another, "vehicles of consciousness." A comment made by Professor Hart in "Six Theories About Apparitions" really sums up the subject matter and conclusions which have been advanced in the last few paragraphs. Discussing a most important aspect of the "problem" of astral projection, Professor Hart remarks upon how it feels to be a phantom by the experiencer of a projection. He lists thirty-nine characteristics reported by those who have undergone separation from their physical bodies. This list is a great contribution to our understanding of astral projection and apparitions.

Knowledge of how it feels to have projected from one's body and to function as a conscious "spirit" separated from the flesh will be gained by reading the various works of Dr. Crookall, which provide a vast collection of projection cases.

In illustration of the principle that phantoms resulting from the mechanisms of astral projection upon occasion display that they are conscious "entities," aware to varying degrees of their surroundings and viewers, a few examples will be given.

A typical projection apparition is described in the *Journal*: S.P.R., August, 1885 (L 2318). The account of Miss Ruth Paget tells how, when she went to the kitchen to draw some water, she saw the figure of her brother, who was away at sea, approaching her. In surprise, Miss Paget asked how he had managed to be there, and he replied in what she described as his normal voice that she was not to say that he was at her home. He was wearing his uniform, and his coat and cap were glistening with water. After this brief communication, the figure vanished. Miss Paget remarks that so realistic was the appearance of her brother that she actually thought he was present in bodily form.

Approximately three months after this phantasmic visitation, her brother returned home. In reply to a most "natural" and harmless (from the standpoint of the psychical researcher) question as to whether he had had any "adventures," he said that he had fallen into the water once when returning to his ship and nearly drowned.

Miss Paget then asked him what the date was when this happened, and his answer revealed that the accident had occurred on the same date that his apparition had been seen.

Curiously, Miss Paget saw her brother's phantom about two hours before the accident took place.

Disregarding the strange anomaly of the time discrepancy for the moment, and in an admittedly arbitrary manner, we must note that the projection-phantom gave every indication that "it" was at least partially aware of Miss Paget, and therefore possessed some measure of consciousness.

A case included in the *Journal*: A.S.P.R., October, 1954, is used by Professor Hart in his paper, "ESP Projection: Spontaneous Cases and the Experimental Method," as an illustration of a deliberately induced experience. However, this example serves equally well as a case of a projection apparition displaying awareness.

During November, 1938, Mr. Lawrence Apsey decided that he would attempt to visit his mother by paranormal means. After a very brief period of willing that he would be seen by her at 12:30 a.m. (his period of concentration took place at 11:15 p.m.), he apparently rested in his bed until the designated hour. At that time he suddenly saw his mother sitting on her bed dressed in an oddly fitting nightgown.

The following morning Mr. Apsey described his curious experience to his wife and at the same time had her inspect notations which he had made immediately following the incident.

Mr. Apsey's mother spoke to his wife the same morning and spontaneously stated that she had seen a phantasmic figure at 12:30 a.m. Later, when she visited Mr. Apsey's apartment, she said that during the night she was awakened by a figure leaning over her bed looking very closely at her face. Oddly, she stated that the figure did not look like her son, for its hair was blond, unlike her son's. She was wearing, she said, a badly fitting nightdress which was the same color as the one Mr. Apsey had seen during his experience. The entire incident was further verified by Mr. Apsey's wife, who provided a written statement that the events as described did take place.

Including this experience in the category of astral projection, which it gives every indication of having been, a degree of awareness on the part of the apparition is shown in that it bent over the percipient as though it had sought her out. When this feature is added to the observations of Mr. Apsey, awareness of surroundings and self, to a large degree, are clearly indicated.

A very important example of a projection apparition, again of earlier years, is described in the *Journal*: S.P.R., December, 1905, and is nicely documented. Essentially, Miss I. M. Pagan woke one night to feel a strange weight pressing on her. When she opened her eyes and looked up, she saw her sister floating above her, covered with a bed cover and with her eyes shut as though sleeping. Miss Pagan attempted to rise and assist her sister but found that she could not do so, for she was held in the grip of a feeling of sleep and she could not open her eyes. Naturally, it will immediately be noted that, according to her description, she had looked up and saw her sister, but in spite of this apparent discrepancy, she felt she was perfectly aware of her room, the placement of the furniture, etc., and felt that she was normally conscious. Finally, Miss Pagan reached out and brought her sister's "body" to her side on the bed. She wrote that the form felt extraordinarily light and seemed to float lightly in the air. After she had performed this action, she fell asleep. She woke once more, spoke to her sister beside her, and went back to sleep again.

The following morning she was told by her sister that she had seen Miss Pagan "astrally" come into her room in an attempt to aid her.

The narrator significantly notes that she and her sister have, on occasion, shared dreams, which is a most important point. Professor Hart has called special attention to this phenomenon. He points out that in such experiences an immaterial "world" which can be experienced is displayed. This phenomenon occupies, I think, a halfway point between telepathy and astral projection.

At any rate, this curiously mixed, almost muddled incident strongly implies a form of astral projection and indicates that self-awareness and consciousness of the surroundings were present even though in a somewhat limited sense.

These very few examples will suffice to illustrate that astral projection apparitions, on occasion, have varying degrees of awareness and are "vehicles of consciousness." Of course, this characteristic in no way implies that projection and projection apparitions do not exist which are devoid of consciousness. A study of the literature of this subject will soon show that projection is frequently unaccompanied by awareness.

The odd appearance of projection phantoms and phantoms in general, the appearance of coverings, etc., and, in fact, the very wearing of clothes has often been the source of much puzzlement and even ridicule. Even Ambrose Bierce wrote a short piece on the nature of ghosts (which he believed did not exist) and expressed his thought that the idea of ghosts' wearing clothes proved that they could not possibly represent anything of a factual nature. The fact that apparitions have been seen with odd accompanying features—and clothes—in no way demonstrates that they were merely the product of an overwrought imagination or a resolute credulity. This characteristic is fully explained by the mechanisms of their "structure," and has been covered by Dr. Robert Crookall and Hornell Hart. In fact, in *The Next World—and the Next*, Dr. Crookall devotes a major section to the problem, if one wishes to call it that, of "ghost clothes." This subject will be discussed in the next chapter.

To conclude, it can be stated that apparitions of all description—those of the dying, the dead, and those resulting from a process of astral projection—show, in some cases, that they in varying degrees possess consciousness of themselves and of their surroundings.

CHAPTER FOURTEEN

A THEORY

OF APPARITIONS

A REVIEW of the significant theories attempting to explain fully the behavior of apparitions is given in Professor Hart's "Six Theories About Apparitions" and, after examining the various concepts which have been advanced over the years, he presents what he calls a modified "etheric-object" theory.

This theory avoids the difficulties inherent in attempts to explain phantasms and does accommodate nicely their many characteristics. Further, it meshes well into the over-all schematic which has been postulated by Dr. Robert Crookall. This last theory, which was touched upon in an earlier chapter, will be reviewed once more.

The revised etheric-object theory assumes first that all objects including living creatures have an etheric double, a psychical duplicate. It also assumes that etheric objects can be brought into being by an imaginative process. And here we have the old concept of "thought-forms."

Etheric objects exist in a psychical space and not in our physical world, but both spaces, as Professor Hart puts it, in certain conditions may merge into each other and act on each other.

Objects of an etheric nature possess the usual three dimensions as well as a time dimension but these four dimensions may not be, at times, "coordinated" with those of our universe.

Many characteristics of etheric objects, the clothes worn by phantoms, for instance, or the visitation of a phantom to a particular person, can be caused by an association of thoughts or by personal attractions such as family ties.

The degree of reality can be charted, in a sense, on a scale which ranges from apparitions unreal and dreamlike, to apparitions normal in appearance, collectively viewed and semiphysical in structure. In other words, nonrealistic phantasms can be the creation of an imaginative process capable of creating apparitional "etheric objects" of great variety. Professor Hart preferred to replace previous telepathic concepts with his theory and insisted that it accommodated all data and explained difficulties encountered with previous hypotheses.

A living person can utilize an etheric duplicate of his physical body as a container for his consciousness, and with this hypothesis astral projection is described. "Double consciousness" can exist in that the consciousness can shift from physical body to etheric double (astral body) and back again in rapid alternation. Presumably, this shifting of consciousness explains how a person who has projected from a "vacated" body can watch it still perform normal operations.

I cannot quite agree with this suggestion, however, because those who have reported experiencing double consciousness have not said that they experienced a shifting from one "body" to another, but did state that, for example, they saw from both "etheric" eyes as well as from their physical eyes.

Actually, Professor Hart's theory is a very sophisticated elaboration of the traditional spiritualist and occult doctrine of an "etheric" world, and accompanying "etheric" duplications ranging from human forms to objects such as chairs and tables. It is an interesting fact that the circle has turned on itself, and, as Dr. Crookall observed, contemporary, sophisticated theories pertaining to various psychical activities were long ago anticipated in mediumistic communications.

For example, a comparatively late version (chronologically speaking) of the thought form/etheric object concept is given in *Other-World People* (Psychic Book Club) by J. W. Herries. It should be mentioned that essentially the persona theory advanced in Professor Hart's *Enigma of Survival* is a sophisticated version of the traditional theosophical/spiritualistic thought-form theory. Herries refers in his book (which bears no date but, since it discusses the famed voice mediums, the Moore sisters, and a series of sittings undertaken after their séances at the British College of Psychic Science featuring communications from "W. T. Stead," which took place about 1931, must have been written not too long afterward) to the idea that persons described by mediums clairvoyantly are actually mental pictures implanted by a telepathic process by spirits in forms recognizable to the sitters, and to the suggestion that they also might be thought-forms created by spirits for the same purpose.

At the moment I do not see why, side by side with the mechanisms advanced by Professor Hart, a telepathic origin for a certain class of apparitions cannot exist—even admitting that, in theory, the revised etheric-object hypothesis includes such phantasms. It does not matter whether one wishes to accept the theory that telepathy represents a transmission from mind to mind which is then transformed by a subconscious process into hallucinations of sight, hearing, touch, etc., or a field theory which assumes that an interacting paranormal "field" exists between people at all times. However, it must again be stated that Professor Hart prefers to replace previous telepathic theories with his own highly developed concept.

As has been observed, apparitions frequently display very "physical" traits. They have been seen collectively; they are seen according to correct principles of perspective and parallax; they produce physical phenomena on occasion such as raps, knockings, pressure; they move objects (phenomena of a thoroughly objective nature); and have been perceived by animals before their human companions realized that they were present.

To refer to the all-inclusive and all-powerful and, to my mind, very unconvincing system of hallucination theorized by G. N. M. Tyrrell for a moment, such characteristics cannot be reasonably accommodated by his concept without placing oneself in the position of logically admitting that it is impossible to distinguish living people from purely imaginary or telepathically induced hallucinations. If one really believed this theoretical scheme, then one could easily be forced into the position of extreme solipsism, admitting that the only thing that can be known for sure is the fact of one's own consciousness. It is true that such a view can be advanced and cannot be refuted, but by the same token an actual believer in such a scheme would be insane.

Inasmuch as apparitions have shown some objective characteristics and at the same time have displayed features which do not reflect physical reality, a theory such as that given by Professor Hart must meet these apparent discrepancies. His schematic does just that. However, a general theory which has been offered by Dr. Crookall agrees with that of Professor Hart but gives a concrete description of the actual mechanisms of apparitions caused by astral projection and apparitions of the dead. This theory was referred to in an earlier chapter but will, of necessity, be outlined again. Dr. Crookall's theory will accept the existence of telepathically created phantoms as a separate phenomenon.

It has, of course, been noted by many researchers that the appearance of apparitions falls off with an increase of time from the moment of death. Professor Flammarion in *Death and Its Mystery: After Death* wrote that he wished to present a diagram which represented the frequency of apparitions relative to time before death, at the moment of death, and after death. This diagram shows that the vast majority of apparitions occur at the moment of death, and it was only after studying comparisons in the thousands that his conclusions were charted.

F. W. H. Myers wrote that phantoms are experienced in increasing number as time grows closer to the moment of death and decrease with lengthening time after death. He notes that after a year's time apparitions appear only very sporadically.

In *Thirty Years of Psychical Research*, Professor Charles Richet wrote that, a very few days after the moment of death, the frequency of apparitions decreases rapidly.

In *The Supreme Adventure*, Dr. Crookall includes an extremely interesting and useful diagram which charts various characteristics of apparitions and communications in relation to periods before, at the moment of, and after death. He particularly notes that physical characteristics, semiobjective qualities, are most prominent near or at the moment of death.

The characteristic of apparitions to be more prevalent at the time of death can be accepted as an established fact beyond reasonable objection.

A vastly important discovery made by Dr. Robert Crookall is that the experiences of those who insist that they have astral projection from their bodies demonstrate that projection which takes place naturally and spontaneously differs from what he calls enforced projection, caused by blows, shock, anaesthetics, and so on. A far greater percentage of those who have experienced natural projection found that they had apparently entered a "world" which in many ways is quite similar to our earth, is very beautiful, extremely enjoyable, and in every way superior to our normal existence. Natural projectors also report seeing friends and relatives who have died and experience what is termed "supernormal consciousness." On the other hand, those who have experienced enforced projection frequently encountered what Dr. Crookall entitles "Hades," or an inferior environmental state with a clouded, dreamlike state of consciousness.

Dr. Crookall accepts the traditional concept that we not only consist of a physical body but also have a duplicate nonphysical body (the soul body) and that we possess another substance which is semiobjective and composed of "ectoplasm" which is responsible for the physical phenomena of spontaneous and mediumistic psychism. This substance is termed the "vehicle of vitality."

According to this schematic, "astral" bodies can be divided into three categories. They may consist of the "vehicle of vitality," which is ideoplastic or capable of transformation by thought as well as being semiobjective. They may be completely nonphysical, containing no trace of the "vehicle of vitality" and are termed the soul body. Or they can be a mixture of both, which can vary in degree.

When the projected double consists only of the "vehicle of vitality" it is not conscious, and when it is seen as an apparition its behavior is nonintelligent and can be classed as a ghostly automaton.

Projected doubles having a large percentage of ectoplasmic substance can, on occasion, create raps or move objects, but in certain cases cannot pass through physical barriers such as walls as do so many reported apparitions. Other projection apparitions, due to the possession of a lesser percentage of the ectoplasmic "vehicle of vitality," can pass through solid matter and are not limited by our earthly environment.

Dr. Crookall has discovered by his analysis of cases that individuals who have mediumistic tendencies more easily extrude astral doubles which contain a larger percentage of ectoplasmic substance than do those extruded by people of nonmediumistic natures. This material frequently appears as a mist or smoke or even a watery substance. Those of nonmediumistic nature do not report seeing this substance when projected.

Dr. Crookall observes that this vaporous substance is, in reality, a part of the ectoplasmic "vehicle of vitality" and comments that its presence dims the awareness of the "soul body," which is the vehicle of consciousness. As a result, this dimming or shrouding of the consciousness is necessarily accompanied by an equally enshrouding dreamlike "Hades" environment.

It must also be mentioned that the misty substance seen by those with mediumistic tendencies during projection experiences has also been seen by those watching the dying. This phenomenon many times appears as a misty, smoky cloud which leaves the body of a dying person and sometimes has been seen to form into a duplicate of the physical body which it has left.

Essentially, Professor Hart's observations found in his "Six Theories About Apparitions," which he titled hypothetical propositions, were statistically analyzed and validated and blend perfectly into the theoretical mechanisms proposed by Dr. Crookall. The first proposition states that complete astral projection, or, as he calls it, ESP projection, involves a self-aware, conscious apparition of a living subject containing memory and deliberate intention which is capable of returning to the physical form with normal memories of actions accomplished. Modify this principle with Crookall's concept of the "vehicle of vitality" with its consciousness-dimming characteristics and the varying quantities of extruded ectoplasmic material accompanying the "soul body," and a very complete theoretical schematic is obtained.

Professor Hart's second proposition is that, as statistically demonstrated, conscious astral-projection apparitions are practically identical to apparitions extruded by the dying and by the dead. Again, Dr. Crookall's observations and Professor Hart's findings are in complete agreement and complement each other.

The third proposition concludes with the statement that, as a result of these verified observations, a percentage of apparitions of the dead must contain memories and intention representative of themselves when living, and provide evidence of spirits who have survived the shock of death. Again, both psychists have advanced identical propositions.

To very briefly reexamine and outline the principles stated, we consist of a physical body, a semiphysical "vehicle of vitality" of ectoplasmic substance capable of limited physical acts but devoid of intelligence in itself, and a "soul body" which is nonphysical and contains our conciousness. At death this mixture of the "vehicle of vitality" and "soul body," in varying combinations according to certain conditions, is extruded from the physical body. After fluctuating periods of time, the enshrouding, consciousness-dimming "vehicle of vitality" dissipates and the "soul body" continues its existence with full awareness.

During illness and other spontaneous processes (natural projection) or by shocks, anaesthetics, etc. (enforced projection), an astral double may be extruded which contains varying degrees of ectoplasmic substance. When it contains a large percentage of this material, objective apparitions are encountered and physical phenomena may occur.

As time after death lengthens, the ectoplasmic substance shrouding the surviving "soul body" begins to dissipate according to governing conditions, and consequently apparitional appearances become fewer and fewer.

The problem posed by apparently impossible elements such as clothes worn by the person when living and apparitions of accompanying animals which are known to be alive, etc., can be resolved when it is remembered that the "vehicle of vitality" is ideoplastic—capable of being molded by thought. Consequently, apparitions of an improbable or even

a ridiculous nature can be formed by the confused consciousness of the newly dead and can, for example, represent last
thoughts or desires strongly held.

This general concept can exist harmoniously with the older
telepathic theories, if one wishes to retain them, and again, in
essence, does not differ from Professor Hart's modified
etheric-object concept.

Professor Hart points out in "Scientific Survival Research"
that Dr. Crookall's data are verified by several orders of legitimate evidence. He notes that the great number of cases
which have now been published fall into an over-all, primary
pattern. This pattern in turn is composed of many other significant characteristics. Attention is drawn to the fact that
accounts of astral projections are not restricted to a limited
area but are found throughout the world and have been reported in long past eras as well as in the present.

The extremely important point is made that many projectors have had their experiences before they had knowledge
that projection existed. Young children have reported this
phenomenon.

The discovery by Dr. Crookall that cases of enforced projection differ in several vital ways from natural projections is
of the utmost importance and could not have been anticipated by those who have claimed to have projected from
their bodies. The fact that those who experience natural projections report that they generally encounter "Paradise" conditions or a state greatly superior to that of normal life, and
the fact that enforced projectors have experienced dreamlike,
confused, and earthlike surroundings could not have been
anticipated beforehand.

CHAPTER FIFTEEN

FINAL

THOUGHTS

APPARITIONS are one of a number of facets of psychical phenomena, all of which combine to form a self-consistent, vast mosaic of paranormal phenomena which in turn are best interpreted in terms of a survival theory. It is undoubtedly true that many psychical manifestations do not imply surviving spirits, but this implication does not suggest that all psychical phenomena are a result of paranormal forces emanating from the living only.

At first glance, most psychical effects directly imply that surviving spirits are, in various ways, directly behind them as a motivating force. Apparitions, as is easily seen, are by their very nature representations of either extruded spirits of the living, astral projections, or representations of surviving spirits of the dead.

However, apparitions both of the living and of the dead must always be considered in terms of their relationship to other forms of psychism, to mediumistic communications, to "physical" phenomena both spontaneous and deliberately induced, to general haunting/poltergeist phenomena, and to the special class of mediumistic communications called cross-correspondences.

When this vast psychical sphere is surveyed, the only explanation capable of accommodating all facets of this subject is the survival theory. Counter-theories such as the so-called super-ESP hypothesis are so overelaborate and forced that they become rivals for the title of Deity. Further, counter-theories ignore certain types of phenomena such as astral projection which, if accepted, can only be interpreted in survivalistic terms.

To paraphrase Professor Hart's conclusion in his extraordinary paper, "Scientific Survival Research," the antisurvivalist must now offer equally valid and detailed evidence for his position as has the survivalist. The burden of proof no longer rests on the shoulders of those who insist that survival of death is verified by all present evidence. The antisurvivalist must offer equally valid evidence before his position can now merit serious attention.

In my opinion, and in the opinion of many parapsychologists of the past and the present, survival of death has been amply demonstrated by the vast amount of evidence now available, and apparitions are one of the several facets of psychism demonstrating this proposition.